Smart Start
for Your Baby

*Your Baby's Development
Week by Week
during the First Year
and How You Can Help*

Penny Warner

💮Meadowbrook Press
Distributed by Simon & Schuster
New York

Library of Congress Cataloging-in-Publication Data

Warner, Penny.

Smart start for your baby: your baby's development week by week during the first year and how you can help / Penny Warner.

p. cm.

Includes index.

ISBN 0-88166-404-9 (Meadowbrook) ISBN 0-7432-2346-2 (Simon & Schuster)

1. Infants—Care. 2. Child development. 3. Child care. 4. Child rearing. I. Title.

RJ61 .W295 2001

649'.122—dc21

2001044468

Editorial Director: Christine Zuchora-Walske

Editor: Joseph Gredler

Production Manager: Paul Woods

Desktop Publishing: Danielle White

Cover Photo: © Jim Cummins/Corbis Stock Market

Index: Beverlee Day

© 2001 by Penny Warner

Published by Meadowbrook Press, 5451 Smetana Drive, Minnetonka, Minnesota 55343

www.meadowbrookpress.com

BOOK TRADE DISTRIBUTION by Simon & Schuster, a division of Simon and Schuster, Inc., 1230 Avenue of the Americas, New York, New York 10020

05 04 03 02 01   10 9 8 7 6 5 4 3 2 1

Printed in the United States of America

Dedication

To Matthew and Rebecca,
the inspiration for everything I do.

Contents

Introduction

Welcome to life with your new baby! The first year of development is an exciting time. Your baby grows faster during this time than any other except his nine months in the womb, making rapid and remarkable gains in all areas of development:

- **Physical Development:** This includes your baby's overall growth; his increasing weight and height; his changing body; the fine motor movements of his hands and fingers; the gross motor movements of his arms, legs, and body; his five senses and how he uses them; and his mobility (how he moves from place to place).

- **Cognitive Development:** This includes your baby's innate intelligence, his thinking ability, his problem-solving skills, his understanding of cause and effect, his memory, his expressive language (how he vocalizes and says words), and his receptive language (how he understands speech and gestures).

- **Psychological Development:** This includes your baby's innate personality and temperament, his ability to socialize, his emotional expressions, his self-awareness, and his self-esteem.

Your baby's amazing achievements may seem almost invisible to you at first, but the observant parent quickly learns to recognize each exciting step. And each new step leads to another amazing milestone. It doesn't take long for your nearly helpless infant to develop into a walking, talking, independent person with emerging social skills, budding intelligence, and a unique personality.

Most babies follow a general pattern of development, reaching certain milestones at certain times. However, each baby's development is unique, so don't be discouraged if your baby doesn't demonstrate a certain ability at the time suggested in this book. You should talk to your pediatrician if your baby is consistently delayed in reaching major milestones.

To help you track your baby's first year, I've designed a fifty-two-week guide that describes all areas of infant development in an easy-to-follow, step-by-step format. In addition, I've suggested an activity or game you can play with your baby to enhance his development at each stage. These tips are simple, positive, entertaining ways to help your baby grow.

You may notice some repetition in the suggested activities, but remember that your baby changes so rapidly that each stage offers something new to observe. For example, let's say you give your baby a stuffed animal when he's only a few weeks old. You'll notice that he plays with the stuffed animal four different ways at four different stages of the first year:

- At one month your baby will mostly look at the stuffed animal, especially if it's brightly colored, interesting, and nearby. He'll be attracted primarily to the visual aspects of the toy.

- At six months your baby will probably try to put part of the stuffed animal in his mouth in an attempt to learn more about it. This oral exploration will tell him the size, temperature, texture, and other details of the toy.

- At nine months your baby will probably grasp, throw, drop, or bang the stuffed animal. He'll be using his fine and gross motor skills to enjoy the toy.

- At twelve months your baby will carry the stuffed animal around and show initial nurturing behavior toward it. Such symbolic play will be appropriate for this age.

Your baby loves repetition and learns by building on previous experiences, so be sure to repeat many of the activities. And always remember: Your baby's favorite plaything is YOU!

Week 1: Awakening

 ## Baby's Physical Development

Growing Body: The average newborn weighs between six and nine pounds, but surprisingly seems to gain no weight during the first week. Babies normally lose some of their birth weight (five to ten percent) due to fluid loss, but they usually gain it back by the second week. By the end of the first year, your baby will have tripled her birth weight!

Sensory Awareness: Your baby uses all five senses from the moment she's born. She looks at your face, listens to your voice, smells your scent, feels your touch, and tastes your skin. That's how she learns about you, and through you she learns about her world.

Feeding: Your baby's first task in life is learning to nurse. She has a rooting reflex to help her find the nipple, a sucking reflex to help her latch on, and a swallowing reflex to help her get milk into her tummy.

 ## How You Can Help

Growing Body: Don't be obsessive about weighing your baby to make sure she's growing properly. Just check to see if she's producing eight to twelve wet diapers a day and having a bowel movement at least every other day. You can usually tell just by looking at her that she's healthy and growing normally.

Sensory Awareness: As your baby's senses develop, provide her with objects that stimulate her sensory awareness. Show her colorful and moving items to look at, such as people, animals, and mobiles. Play musical toys or sing songs to stimulate her listening skills. Give her various textures to feel, such as a soft blanket, a firm toy, a pliable teether, and a furry stuffed animal.

Feeding: Feed your baby in a comfortable place with lots of pillows for support. Use this time to talk, sing, caress, and make eye contact with her. Feeding time promotes both physical growth and social development.

Baby's Cognitive Development

Thinking: Visual stimulation is one of the primary ways your baby begins to use her brain. Her vision is only 20/200 at birth, so she sees better at close range. She's able to track your finger at a distance of eight inches, she can distinguish faces from other patterns, and she can see bright distinctive colors such as red and green.

Language: Your baby communicates with you long before she uses recognizable words. Her facial expressions often reveal basic emotions, her hands express some of her needs, and her body language sometimes tells you how she's feeling and what she wants. If you take the time to learn her cues, you'll be able to satisfy her needs efficiently.

Problem Solving: Although you solve most of your baby's problems in the early weeks, she uses reflexes to solve some problems on her own. She shivers to keep warm, burrows to find an air pocket, and startles to remind you to handle her carefully. She also solves the problem of getting fed by rooting and eventually crying.

 # How You Can Help

Thinking: Begin playing Peek-a-Boo with your baby during nursing or holding time. While smiling and talking to her, cover your face with a cloth. Continue talking to her, then remove the cloth and smile. Watch her eyes widen as you magically reappear.

Language: Just because your baby isn't speaking doesn't mean she isn't learning language. The more you talk to her, the sooner she'll develop language skills. As you talk to your baby, use a high-pitched voice, simple words, short sentences, lots of repetition, and facial expressions. Watch her respond with eye contact and body language such as kicking her legs and flapping her arms.

Problem Solving: To help your baby learn to solve problems even at this early age, give her simple choices. For example, put a rattle in one of her hands and a soft cloth in her other hand. See what she does with the objects on a very basic level. She may shake one and ignore the other, drop one and focus on the other, or try to put both objects in her mouth. You can also place a nipple near her mouth and watch her figure out how to get it.

Baby's Psychological Development

Self-Awareness: In the first few weeks your baby seems to think she's still attached to you as one long extension of your breast. However, she will begin to find her hands and feet, feel the discomfort of separation from her parents, and possibly bond with a special blanket or lovey even at this early age. These experiences will promote her self-awareness.

Emotional Expression: Before your baby learns to express her needs and emotions through recognizable words, she expresses them through vocalizations. Her cries may differ from one another as she tries to communicate her feelings, so listen carefully to these signals. You may hear a whimpering cry when she's waking up, a complaining cry when she's wet, a vigorous cry when she's hungry, and a hysterical cry when she's in great distress.

Social Interaction: Bonding is a baby's early emotional and physical attachment to her parents. It's achieved through parents' naming, touching, holding, feeding, and taking care of their baby. A baby needs to bond with her parents in order to thrive and feel loved, safe, and secure.

 # How You Can Help

Self-Awareness: To help your baby begin to distinguish herself from the world, give her some time in front of a mirror. At first she'll merely wonder at the movement and face in front of her. However, she'll soon realize through cause and effect that she's the person causing the movement. Few things delight a baby more than her reflection.

Emotional Expression: Most experts believe that if you respond to your baby's cries quickly, she's likely to cry less and feel more secure because she knows someone is taking good care of her. The old adage "Let her cry it out" is no longer accepted by most experts.

Social Interaction: Spend as much time with your baby as you like. Ignore the old-fashioned admonition that you'll spoil your baby if you pick her up and hold her too much. You can't spoil your baby in the first year. In fact, the more you pick her up and hold her, the more rapidly she develops physically, cognitively, and psychologically.

Week 2: Reflexes

 ## Baby's Physical Development

Reflexes: Your baby has a number of involuntary reflexes that help keep him alive, such as breathing, sucking, swallowing, and shivering. Some of these, like rooting and startling, disappear over time. Others (standing, stepping, swimming, and grasping) are the foundation for motor skills your baby will learn later.

Gross Motor Skills: The larger body movements (using torso, arms, and legs) develop from your baby's reflexes. For example, the stepping reflex will eventually lead to walking. The swimming reflex will eventually lead to crawling. Laying your baby on his tummy with his head to one side gives him the opportunity to turn it to the other side. This helps him learn to lift his head, and it stimulates left-right coordination.

Fine Motor Skills: The skills that require small muscles involve primarily the hands and fingers, and to some extent the feet and toes. These muscles take longer to master, but you may notice your baby's initial attempts to control his hands and fingers as he tries to swipe at the air in front of him, grasp a rattle, or entwine his fingers in your hair.

 ## How You Can Help

Reflexes: There are certain activities you can do to enhance your baby's reflexes. To help him with sucking and swallowing, stroke his cheek. He'll move his head in search of the nipple. To minimize his startle reflex, use a soft voice, pick him up slowly, and don't make sudden movements or noises.

Gross Motor Skills: To encourage your baby to practice pre-crawling skills, lay him on his tummy. Get down on your stomach, face him, and start talking to him. He may try to lift his head as he flaps his arms and legs. Move from one side to his other to encourage him to turn his head left and right.

Fine Motor Skills: You can help your baby begin to control his fine motor movements by gently massaging his tight finger grasp. To encourage this grasp, place a rattle in his hand and watch him curl his fingers around the handle. Gently uncurl his fingers to help him release the rattle.

Baby's Cognitive Development

Senses: Child development specialist Jean Piaget studied children's cognitive skills and found that the development of intelligence begins at birth. Your baby learns about his environment through his senses and by using his motor skills. His reflexive motor responses are the first step in this rapid cognitive growth.

Language: Although your baby doesn't speak or gesture deliberately yet, you can see him trying to communicate with you if you watch him closely. He's beginning to express himself through meaningful noises such as cooing, gurgling, and clicking his tongue and facial expressions such as smiling and frowning. He will fine-tune these skills rapidly over time.

Visual Stimulation: One of the most important ways a baby learns is through vision. As your baby begins to see his world more clearly, he begins to organize objects based on color, size, and especially movement. He needs plenty of colorful, exciting things to look at as his vision improves over the next several weeks.

 # How You Can Help

Senses: To help your baby learn from the moment he's born, stimulate his senses and watch him respond. For example, move a brightly colored object across his field of vision, and he'll try to follow it with his eyes. Call his name, and he'll try to turn his head in the direction of the sound. Touch his palm, and he'll grasp.

Language: As your baby begins to express his needs and wants, reinforce his sounds and expressions by imitating them. If he coos, coo back. If he purses his lips, reflect the expression in your face. Then add new sounds and faces and watch him try to copy you. You're building the foundation of communication.

Visual Stimulation: To encourage your baby's cognitive development, make his world visually interesting. Place colorful pictures on the walls and ceiling near his crib. Hang mobiles that move, make sounds, and are visually stimulating. Change them occasionally to hold his interest. Walk around the house and show him fun things to see.

Baby's Psychological Development

Recognizing Mom: A baby begins to recognize his mother's face as early as the second week or sooner. Child development experts have studied babies' reactions to different faces, and they've confirmed that mothers' faces produce excitement, pleasure, and calm. If dad is the primary caregiver, he'll be the one baby recognizes first.

Responding to Dad: Although mom is often the primary caregiver, today's dad is much more involved in baby's care than ever before. Men are just as capable of satisfying babies' needs as women, but they usually respond to babies differently. While moms tend to caress, murmur, or sing to their babies, dads tend to move babies' arms and legs, zoom their bodies through the air, or tickle their tummies.

Attachment: The close emotional bond between parents and baby begins at birth (and some say in the uterus). It occurs naturally through touch, talk, and eye contact. Attaching to your baby is one of the most important ways of developing his confidence and security so he can learn and thrive.

 # How You Can Help

Recognizing Mom: Continue playing Peek-a-Boo to enhance your baby's recognition of you. Place your baby on your lap, facing you, then cover your face with a handkerchief or washcloth. Talk to him through the cloth for a moment or two, then remove the cloth and say, "Peek a boo!" Watch his face!

Responding to Dad: Make sure dad is actively involved in baby's daily care to reinforce your baby's emotional attachment to him. Dad can change diapers, give baths, and feed with bottles (either expressed breast milk or formula). Encourage dad to enjoy the special moments that occur frequently throughout the day with your baby.

Attachment: To enhance your baby's sense of attachment, cuddle and hold him often, talk to him throughout the day, and simply sit and look at him. If you take care of your baby's needs as soon as they appear, he will learn to trust not only you, but others in his environment and in his life.

Week 3: Attachment

 ## Baby's Physical Development

Hearing Voices: We now know that babies can hear in the womb, although the sounds are muffled. They can distinguish between music and conversation, loud and soft, and different rhythms of speech such as reading aloud and chatting. A baby can recognize her mother's voice by three weeks of age, if not sooner, and prefers this voice to others.

Touch Time: Your baby's sense of touch is especially acute during the first month of life. She loves to be caressed, massaged, and carried close to your body. The positive effects of gentle touch increase her development in all areas. If you accidentally pinch or prick her during a diaper change, she will react momentarily by screaming, but the memory of the pain will fade quickly.

Kicking Legs: Your baby's leg movements are gaining momentum as she learns to manipulate her large muscles. You'll sometimes find her kicking while she's lying on her back, when you pick her up, and even when you put her in the bath. Watch out for splashing water!

 ## How You Can Help

Hearing Voices: You can enhance your baby's ability to recognize your voice by reading to her from picture books that offer short sentences, rhyming words, and repetitive phrases. She's too young to understand the content, but she's not too young to enjoy the sounds and patterns of language. Also, research shows that early reading correlates to interest in reading later on.

Touch Time: Place your baby face-up on a soft padded blanket on the floor. Lightly cover your hands with unscented, non-allergenic lotion, and give her a massage. Start at her shoulders, work down to her fingers, then move down her torso to her feet. Roll her over and repeat.

Kicking Legs: Lay the whirling dervish on her back, grasp her lower legs gently, and begin a cycling movement. Also gently move her legs forward, backward, up and down, back and forth, and even like a frog. Be creative, but don't be too vigorous. After each new movement, release her legs to see if she tries to copy the movement.

Baby's Cognitive Development

Perceptual Development: As soon as your baby begins looking at and listening to the world, she starts building her perceptual skills. She acquires information through her senses and she slowly starts to categorize objects based on simple traits such as softness, hardness, flatness, roundness, rigidity, and flexibility. As she learns, her expectations of an object help her make even finer distinctions.

Cause and Effect: Your baby learns the basics of cause and effect from the simple act of breastfeeding or bottle-feeding. When she's hungry, she cries, which eventually brings the milk. Although crying is initially a reflex, your baby gradually learns to tailor her cry to fit the need. She also learns that sucking vigorously brings more milk, and biting temporarily ends a feeding!

Object Awareness: Your baby is interested primarily in feeding, sleeping, and being cared for. When she learns she's going to be fed regularly, she'll let herself be interrupted briefly during a feeding if something interesting comes along. This demonstrates her expanding awareness of the world around her.

 # How You Can Help

Perceptual Development: Offer your baby dissimilar objects to look at, listen to, and touch. For example, you might show her a flat plate and a round ball, a soft blanket and a rough towel, a cold bottle and a warm bottle, and so on. She's learning concepts through experience and comparison, and she'll soon be able to categorize objects based on shape, color, size, and number.

Cause and Effect: You can help your baby learn about cause and effect while she's feeding. For example, sing to your baby while she nurses. When she pauses, stop singing. Watch her pauses become more frequent as she tries to figure out what causes the singing and what stops it.

Object Awareness: As your baby's curiosity begins to interrupt her habits, you'll find wonderful opportunities to introduce her to new and exciting objects for study. For example, attach something new to the mobile over her crib and watch her body language. Show her a new rattle during feeding time, and she may stop nursing for a moment to study the interesting object. Keep her world fresh to stimulate her increasing curiosity.

Baby's Psychological Development

Active Temperament: You can see the foundation of your baby's personality and temperament in the first month. One of her many traits is her activity level, which seems to be innate. Babies who are active in the uterus often move around a lot after they're born. Experts say a baby's activity level will probably remain consistent throughout her life.

Quiet Temperament: If your baby was mostly quiet in the womb, she'll probably be slow to warm up after birth. She may sleep more, make fewer noises, and be an "easy" baby. She may prefer to watch and listen rather than participate.

In Sync: A baby and her parents often learn to be "in sync" in the first few weeks after birth. Parents watch their baby for signs of communication, then attempt to satisfy her needs. This connection between parents and baby is the beginning of a lifelong sensitivity to one another.

 # How You Can Help

Active Temperament: Active babies need more attention to keep them occupied. They tend to stay awake longer, move around more, and cry more easily. Move slowly with an active baby, to give her a sense of calm and to help her learn to control her activity.

Quiet Temperament: If your baby is slow to warm up, meet her needs by letting her approach new situations, people, and experiences at a slower pace. Talk to her, reassure her before trying something new, and respond to her distress if she's uncomfortable.

In Sync: As you begin to understand your baby's needs, moods, and timetable, you realize she is essentially her own person. Pay attention to cues such as eye contact, facial expressions, body movements, and vocalizations. You'll soon be able to read her signals for attention, food, quiet, and stimulation.

Week 4: Awareness

 ## Baby's Physical Development

Speech Sounds: By one month babies begin to notice the difference between similar speech sounds such as "bah" and "pah." Their ability to hear, separate, and distinguish sounds is remarkable at such a young age. Some babies even react to the subtleties of different vowel sounds.

Color Vision: Experts disagree on whether newborns can see color, but most acknowledge that babies can distinguish among red, green, and white by four weeks. Perhaps they only perceive the contrast, but maybe they actually see the colors.

Alertness: Your baby is awake only a small portion of the day, but that time is increasing since birth. Most babies experience several alert periods during the day, usually lasting one-half to one hour. They watch attentively, listen for new sounds, and play with their fingers.

 ## How You Can Help

Speech Sounds: Some babies are especially susceptible to middle-ear infections in infancy. If not treated properly, ear infections can become chronic, causing temporary hearing loss. If your baby misses too many speech sounds in early development due to ear infections, it could impair his ability to learn language. Be sure to have him checked regularly, especially when he has sniffles, rubs his ears, or doesn't seem to be responding to your voice.

Color Vision: Since infants prefer bright solid colors like red and green, give your baby lots of stimulating mobiles, posters, and toys in basic colors. Fine prints and pastels aren't as attractive to him, but he does like bold patterns, familiar shapes, and especially faces. Display pictures of other babies to keep him company.

Alertness: When your baby is fully awake, it's the perfect time to play. He's more apt to stay alert if you provide interesting things for him to look at and listen to. You are especially fun to play with, so try to enjoy this alert time with your baby. A parent is the perfect toy!

Baby's Cognitive Development

Short-Term Memory: Your baby's memory is developing as he learns to recognize sounds, faces, tastes, and smells. He can remember an object if it reappears after two to three seconds. Watch his eyes dilate or his sucking increase as recognition occurs.

Patterns: Your baby begins to settle into patterns around one month. He expects to be fed at regular intervals and he tends to sleep, wake, and even cry at certain times. You can learn his patterns by recording his activities in a baby book.

Playthings: Early learning begins with interaction with simple playthings. Babies learn from watching and manipulating toys that offer a variety of sensory stimulation. Mirrors are especially fun. They help build your baby's self-concept, they offer endless hours of fascination, and they change as your baby grows.

 # How You Can Help

Short-Term Memory: You can help increase your baby's memory by playing a game of Here-It-Is! While holding your baby, bring a brightly colored object into his field of vision. Move the object slightly to attract his attention, then move it out of sight. Wait two to three seconds, then bring it back into his field of vision. Say the object's name to reinforce the connection. Repeat several times.

Patterns: By understanding your baby's patterns, you can be better prepared to meet his needs. If you know it's almost feeding time, you can begin nursing him instead of waiting for him to cry. If you know it's almost naptime, you can begin your ritual of putting him down. If you sense he's about to cry, you can pick him up and soothe him before his tears begin in earnest. When it's alert time, you can be ready with toys.

Playthings: It's not too early to provide simple toys for your baby to study and enjoy. Good playthings for the one-month-old baby include a music box with moveable parts, baby gyms that attach to the crib, mobiles that play music and spin around, unbreakable mirrors, and colorful stuffed animals. Make sure the toys have no sharp edges, no detachable parts, and no strings or cords that can entangle your baby.

Baby's Psychological Development

Eye Contact: Your baby's eye contact is increasing at this time. Earlier he looked primarily at your forehead or hairline, perhaps because of the contrast between your face and hair. But now he's attracted to your eyes, and he's beginning to differentiate parts of your face.

First Smile: The first smile is not always gas, as child experts used to think. This grin may be the beginning of a truly social smile. Experts have documented that first smiles usually appear between four and eight weeks, but many parents are convinced that their babies smile as early as the first day of life.

Sadness: Your baby's first emotion is usually distress caused by hunger, cold, wetness, or loneliness. However, by four weeks your baby can actually feel sad, or at least can be sensitive to sadness. If a parent cries or makes a sad face, a baby may pick up on that emotion and break into tears, too.

 # How You Can Help

Eye Contact: Hold your baby face-to-face and look into his eyes. Talk to him, smile at him, and make funny faces to hold his attention. Watch his face change as your expression changes. Notice that he maintains eye contact longer than he did in the first weeks. Wink at him, blink your eyes slowly, and see if he reacts. Cover your eyes, uncover them, and say, "Peek a boo," to bring his attention back to your eyes.

First Smile: You can encourage your baby's first smile by holding him face-to-face and smiling at him frequently. Talk to him, smile wide, show your teeth, and wiggle your tongue. Make the smile as interesting and attractive as you can. If you think your baby is beginning to smile, reinforce it with a cheery word and a big grin. Sometimes a light stroke on either side of his mouth can produce a smile.

Sadness: Tears or emotional distress from a parent suffering from postpartum depression can have a strong impact on a baby. Be sure to seek help from your doctor if you still have the postpartum blues. You may need counseling and perhaps medication. You don't have to feel sad, and neither does your baby.

Week 5: Watchfulness

 ## Baby's Physical Development

Visual Skills: Your baby is looking all over the place! Her vision isn't 20/20 yet (she's still nearsighted), but it's improving. She can see objects clearly as long as they're about a foot away. She can track objects moving back and forth and she can follow them up and down. Watch her flap her arms and legs excitedly as she spots something new and interesting.

Physical Growth: Your baby has probably grown about one inch since birth, and she's putting on weight even more rapidly. If she looks healthy, is taking milk well, and has alert periods, she's probably doing well. Most infants feed about six times a day, taking in about three ounces of milk each time, but this varies from baby to baby. If she's outgrowing her infant clothes, she's developing!

Voluntary Control: Your baby is gaining more control over her arms. You might see her try to reach for objects in front of her. She's not able to make direct contact easily, but you can celebrate her effort as she attempts eye-hand coordination.

 ## How You Can Help

Visual Skills: As your baby's vision improves, give her more interesting things to look at. Move objects slowly back and forth about twelve inches from her face. Then move them up and down, and see if she can track them. To help her follow the objects, make noise with them, so she has another reason to look at them.

Physical Growth: Your baby should be gaining back the weight she lost in the first week. Check with your doctor to make sure your baby is getting enough milk. Your doctor may suggest increased feedings, especially if your baby is sleeping through mealtimes, which can impair weight gain.

Voluntary Control: As your baby reaches out and tries to grasp objects, make sure some of them are within her reach and easy to hold, such as teething rings, colorful rattles, or small stuffed animals. Move the objects around slightly so she's attracted to them and help her make contact as she reaches for them.

Baby's Cognitive Development

Vocalization: Around this time your baby may begin to vocalize when you talk. She's trying to imitate your speech, and she may be producing ten to fifteen speech-related sounds. Vowels are especially common, since they're easier to say than consonants, which come later.

Overstimulation: Your baby has been out of the womb only a few weeks, and she's still getting used to a stimulating world dramatically different from the dark, insulated womb. Be sure she gets an occasional rest from the excitement, bright lights, and loud sounds. Otherwise she's likely to become overstimulated and irritable.

Tactile Discrimination: Your baby is very sensitive to touch. She responds to differences between hard and soft, cold and warm, and rough and smooth. She loves to be held, caressed, kissed, carried, and handled.

 # How You Can Help

Vocalization: As your baby begins to vocalize, engage her in "conversations." Talk to her, then pause and wait for her to vocalize. When she does, imitate her sounds by using a high-pitched voice and an animated face. The more you repeat her sounds, the more she'll repeat yours.

Overstimulation: You can minimize the risk of overstimulation and irritability by watching your baby's body language, muscle tension, and facial expressions. She'll tell you she's had enough fun by acting fussy, restless, or inattentive.

Tactile Discrimination: Play a tactile game with your baby to help her learn about various textures, temperatures, and sensations. Find objects that are hard and soft, such as a block and a pillow; ones that are smooth and rough, such as a towel and a Velcro strap; and ones that are cool and warm, such as a plastic toy and a hand. Place her on her back, and gently rub the objects on her tummy while talking about them. Watch the reaction in her eyes, face, and body.

Baby's Psychological Development

Activity Cycle: Your baby's temperament continues to reveal itself to you. One aspect that becomes obvious early on is her cycle of activity. Many babies eat, sleep, play, and defecate on a fairly regular schedule. You can practically set your watch by them. Others are less predictable. They wake at various times, eat at irregular intervals, and fill their diapers often or seldom.

Diminishing Crying: After the first month, you should be able to distinguish your baby's different cries. Some of these are vocalizations of her needs and wants. As her cries become more specialized (the wake-up cry, the wet-diaper cry, the hungry cry, the distress cry, and so on), you'll be better able to identify each cry and respond accordingly.

Emotional Connection: Your baby recognizes you by your smell, touch, voice, and face. She needs to spend time being held, carried around in a front pack, touched, and kept close to you. Babies thrive when they have lots of physical contact with their parents. In fact, they can't develop properly without it.

 # How You Can Help

Activity Cycle: You can help your baby regulate her schedule to some degree, although her patterns are generally innate. Follow her schedule for the most part, but you might wake her a little earlier for feeding or playtime, put her down at certain times for naps or bedtime, and help her find some routine if she doesn't seem to have one.

Diminishing Crying: If your baby starts to cry because she's lonely, bored, or irritable, you can often distract her from her fussiness with a funny face, interesting toy, or change of location. If you respond quickly to a fussy cry, you can often prevent a bigger meltdown.

Emotional Connection: Parents spend a large portion of the day caring for their babies' physical and cognitive needs, but they often forget to take time to simply enjoy their babies. Lie down on the floor with your baby on your tummy, so she can feel your warmth, listen to your heartbeat and breathing, and hear your soft voice.

Week 6: Anticipating

 Baby's Physical Development

Sitting with Support: Any day now your baby will begin to sit with support. His head will be less floppy as his neck muscles become stronger. If he's had some exercise time on his tummy, he'll soon be able to watch the world while propped up by pillows, blankets, or an infant seat.

Ready to Roll: Babies sometimes surprise their parents by rolling over in these early weeks. Leaving your baby on an elevated surface without supervision can be dangerous. It only takes a second for him to roll off the changing table, counter, or bed. Never leave him unattended on an elevated surface.

Circular Eye Coordination: As your baby's visual acuity increases, he's able to see things a few inches farther away and track them for longer periods. He may also begin to follow objects that move in a circular pattern, which takes advanced eye coordination.

 How You Can Help

Sitting with Support: Give your baby lots of tummy time, so he can practice lifting and turning his head. To encourage the strengthening of his neck muscles, lie down on the floor with him and move from one side to his other. Also let him sit in his infant seat or on the couch, with receiving blankets and pillows for support. Lap-sitting is great exercise for your baby, too.

Ready to Roll: To help your baby practice rolling over, dress him in a diaper only, if the room is warm enough, or in something he can move easily in. Lay him on his tummy. As his legs curl and his back arches up, give him a lift with your hand. Then tuck his arm under him, and gently roll him over. While he's on his back, help him practice turning back-to-front by gently swinging one of his legs over to the other side and helping his upper body with your other hand.

Circular Eye Coordination: As your baby begins to follow circular movements, you can help develop this ability by holding a brightly colored object about twelve inches from his face. Slowly move the object in a circle, and see if he tries to follow it with his eyes. He probably won't make full circles yet, but this skill will develop rapidly over the next few weeks.

Baby's Cognitive Development

Vocalizing: Your baby is making finer and finer vocalizations. He's also repeating many of the sounds you make, especially vowel sounds. He's probably making four times the amount of sounds he made as a newborn, an amazing increase in both his awareness of vocalizations and his ability to re-create them.

Anticipatory Excitement: Your baby is beginning to anticipate routine activities and organize his previously chaotic world. He may kick his legs when he hears mom's or dad's keys in the door, his eyes may light up when you pick him up for a feeding, and he may vocalize while you talk on the phone.

Binocular Vision: Your baby's brain is beginning to develop the ability to form a single image from the two images produced by his eyes, as long as the objects are at least twelve to fifteen inches away. This is a big improvement over seeing doubled or blurred images.

 # How You Can Help

Vocalizing: As your baby quadruples his speech sounds, you can boost his vocabulary further by repeating his vocalizations and adding more and more sounds. For example, if your baby says, "goo," repeat the sound and then say, "gah" or "gee." Sit where he can watch your mouth as you talk.

Anticipatory Excitement: Try to establish a routine, so your baby can learn to anticipate daily activities. Welcome him with the same morning greeting, and watch his facial expression come alive. Sit in the same place for his feeding, and watch him kick with excitement. Do something different occasionally, and see how he reacts.

Binocular Vision: As your baby's brain works to bring his world into focus, you can enhance his binocular vision by holding an object about ten inches from his face. While he's looking at the object, move it slowly away from his face. Observe how long he focuses on the object, and notice when he looks away. To keep his attention as long as possible, keep the object moving, interesting, colorful, and attractive. Your face is perfect for this!

Baby's Psychological Development

Father Attachment: Attachment to dad is often slower to develop than attachment to mom, since mom is often the primary caregiver. But if dad has been participating in care and play, your baby should be reacting positively to his face and voice by now, more so than to strangers.

Emotion Recognition: Your baby is not only listening and vocalizing more, he's also reading faces and interpreting the emotional qualities of communication. He can distinguish among a happy voice, a sad voice, and an angry voice, and he may respond with a matching facial expression.

Smiling Back: Your baby is probably smiling back at people who smile at him, whether it's mom, dad, friends, or relatives—unless the face is unfriendly, bearded, or masked. Then he's likely to cry!

 # How You Can Help

Father Attachment: If dad is at work all day, make sure he spends plenty of time with your baby when he gets home. Your baby gets a different kind of attention from dad. In addition to being a wonderful plaything, have dad change diapers, give baths, give bottles of breast milk or formula, and take the baby on outings without mom, so their special bond can continue to grow.

Emotion Recognition: Play a game of Funny Voices to enhance your baby's ability to distinguish emotional tones. Choose a simple baby book with lots of facial expressions. Seat your baby on your lap and read the book using funny voices that match the emotions shown on the faces. Your baby is never too young to be read to!

Smiling Back: Seat your baby in your lap facing you. Give him a big smile, and watch him imitate it. Relax your face, then smile again. See if your baby imitates you each time. In a couple of weeks he'll be smiling spontaneously at anything and everything, especially your smiling face!

Week 7: Alertness

 Baby's Physical Development

Visual Skills: Your baby may begin to turn her eyes and head toward an object held at her side but still within her peripheral vision. As she tries to focus on the object, her head may bounce, and she may lose eye contact. But if the object is interesting and attractive, she may make the effort to find it again.

Awake and Asleep: As your baby becomes more alert during the day, she begins to stay awake longer. At the same time, she probably takes longer naps when she finally does go to sleep. Two to three naps a day are common during this period. Her total sleep time will range from eight to fifteen hours.

Reaching: Your baby may reach for items but be unable to grasp them because of clenched fists. Soon she'll begin to open her hands in anticipation of grasping an item. She's making the change from reflexive to adaptive reaching.

 How You Can Help

Visual Skills: As your baby's head control and peripheral vision increase, help her practice locating objects just beyond her field of vision. Find a colorful object, and hold it behind her head. Gradually bring the object around her side toward her front, while moving it up and down slightly. Watch as she notices the object and tries to turn toward it. Hold the object at the spot where she first begins to see it, so she can practice finding it.

Awake and Asleep: You can help extend your baby's wakeful times by making playtime interesting and stimulating. Before feeding her, entertain her with playthings, conversation, and activity. Then play with her some more after she's nursed. If you get tuckered out, let her entertain herself awhile; this will help promote her initiative. She'll usually take a good long nap after an especially interesting playtime.

Reaching: To help your baby open her hand to grasp an object, hold the object near her hand. As she reaches for it, place the object in her closed palm, and gently work her fingers open until she releases her grip and wraps her fingers around the object. After a few minutes, do the same with the other hand.

Baby's Cognitive Development

Syllables: As your baby begins to turn crying sounds into different types of expressions, you may notice that some of her cries sound like syllables such as "gaga" or "nana." These syllables are the foundation of your baby's first words, and they often refer to parents or caregivers.

Visual Stimulation: As your baby's field of vision increases, the pictures in front of her become clearer. She should now be able to focus on an object twenty inches away. This is twice the distance she could see at birth.

Auditory Recognition: Your baby is getting better at recognizing familiar sounds, and she may respond differently to different sounds. She'll pause during nursing or play if she hears a loud or sudden sound, and her eyes will widen with interest. If the sound is soft and interesting, such as a gentle voice or music, she may turn toward the noise. If it's conversation, she may try to imitate it.

 # How You Can Help

Syllables: Help your baby practice making syllables by repeating them back to her when she vocalizes. She'll soon change her cries into more expressive speech sounds. The "ah-ah" sound is one of the easiest to master. Your baby will soon add throat sounds such as "gah" or "kah" and eventually "nah." You'll have fun guessing which word she'll say first.

Visual Stimulation: Hold objects farther away from your baby's eyes (about twenty inches) and watch her try to maintain her focus. She prefers more detail now, so give her interesting and complex objects to look at. She still prefers three-dimensional objects over pictures, but she may respond to vivid photos of items she can recognize.

Auditory Recognition: Play a listening game with your baby to help her distinguish various sounds. Prop her in her infant seat and shake a rattle. Watch her try to locate the sound. Repeat a couple of times, then use a different object to make a noise. Watch your baby's eyes light up as she recognizes the different sound.

Baby's Psychological Development

Expressing Pleasure: Around this time your baby will not only smile at a smiling face, she may also smile when she hears a familiar sound, sees a favorite toy, or recognizes a special friend or relative. Sometimes even a few words or the sight of a dog will elicit a grin from a happy baby.

Body Play: Playtime is taking on a new dimension as your baby discovers her body and plays with her fingers, toes, and mouth. Babies love to watch their hands and kick their legs. They also love to vocalize by gurgling, squealing, blowing bubbles, and playing with their lips, tongue, and saliva.

Socialization: Your baby enjoys company, and strangers are less threatening to her at this age, as long as they aren't too scary looking! She especially enjoys children, and she'll offer new facial expressions to those who talk to her and pay attention to her. Your baby is a social being, and as long as a parent is nearby, she usually enjoys seeing new faces.

 # How You Can Help

Expressing Pleasure: Add to your baby's enjoyment of life by smiling back at her when she grins. When you present something new, show her a pleasant face and talk about the object in a light, happy voice. She'll soon respond with a positive expression. You're helping her learn to be happy by using social referencing. In other words, she's learning to recognize her feelings by checking your reactions first.

Body Play: Set your baby in her infant seat, so she can easily reach her feet and play with her toes and fingers. Set a mirror nearby, so she can watch herself play and increase her sense of self. Then lay her on her back, so she can continue her play from a different angle.

Socialization: Invite some kids over to play with your baby. She'll learn faster from other kids than from anyone else, and she'll enjoy the company and attention. Keep an eye on the kids, so they don't get too wild with your baby and accidentally hurt or upset her.

Week 8: Interacting

 Baby's Physical Development

Grasp and Shake: Although initially inadvertent, shaking a rattle produces a circular response around this age. First your baby realizes the rattle in his hand makes a noise, then he learns that shaking his hand creates the noise from the rattle.

Hand to Mouth: Your baby is bringing his hand to his mouth more voluntarily than reflexively now. Oral exploration is one of the primary ways your baby learns about his world. He's also discovering the pleasure of putting his fingers, hands, or other objects in his mouth.

Heads Up: When your baby is placed on his tummy now, he should be lifting his head regularly. He may even try to get his shoulders off the ground in order to see more things around him. These little pushups are the next step toward crawling.

 How You Can Help

Grasp and Shake: As your baby interacts with his environment, he begins to learn that he has an impact on objects and people. When a rattle is placed in his hand, he learns that he has the power to make noise. Give him different objects to hold and shake, and watch his reactions as the noises change.

Hand to Mouth: Offer your baby lots of interesting things to grasp and explore with his mouth. A rattle is ideal, since it's small, safe, and clean, but other objects offer different information. If your baby puts a dry washcloth in his mouth, he'll discover roughness and dryness. If he puts a chilled teether in his mouth, he'll learn about cold and firmness. If he mouths a small stuffed animal, he'll discover furriness and softness.

Heads Up: As your baby practices raising his head, help him further strengthen his neck muscles by getting down on the floor with him and talking to him face-to-face. This will encourage him to look up. As he does, raise your head higher, and watch him try to imitate you.

Baby's Cognitive Development

Vocalization: Your baby's pre-language skills are developing rapidly. He continues to differentiate vowel and consonant sounds from crying sounds. Identifying these distinct, meaningful sounds is the foundation for speech. Your baby is also becoming aware that, compared to crying, these sounds produce different responses from you.

Visual Tracking: While your baby is already adept at following an object moving from side to side, he's increasing his ability to follow an object moving up and down. This is a big change from newborn vision, which mainly tracked only a few inches horizontally.

Object Permanence: Your baby may suddenly notice when you're out of the room or merely out of sight. Watch his facial expression change when he sees you again. He'll soon begin to fuss when you disappear (thinking you're not coming back), but he'll be overjoyed when he sees you're still there!

 # How You Can Help

Vocalization: When you hear your baby make vowel or consonant sounds, repeat them and further encourage his listening and discrimination skills by adding different sounds. For example, if your baby says, "ga-ga-ga," repeat it, then add, "goo-goo-goo" or "ba-ba-ba." See if he tries to imitate your changes.

Visual Tracking: Increase your baby's capacity for vertical tracking by moving interesting objects up and down in his field of vision. As his head control increases, he's better able to follow an item vertically, since he now moves his head along with his eyes. To keep him interested, occasionally choose a different object.

Object Permanence: To help your baby learn that objects still exist even though they're out of sight, show him an object in his field of vision, then move it out of sight and say, "Where did it go?" Watch to see if he looks for it by moving his eyes or head. Bring it back into view and say, "Here it is!" Watch his response. He'll soon learn that objects don't cease to exist even though they can't be seen.

Baby's Psychological Development

Approach and Withdrawal: As your baby's temperament and personality emerge, you'll begin to notice that he either tends to delight in new situations or seems to pull away. Some babies really enjoy new toys, new people, and new experiences. Others are slow to warm up, like to move with caution, and prefer things to remain the same. A few babies don't seem to show definite preferences.

Developing Trust: As long as your baby's needs are met, he continues to develop trust in his caregivers and environment. Erik Erikson studied how babies respond when their needs for milk, clothes, sleep, play, and nurturing are satisfied. He found that these infants usually grow up to be trusting adults who interact confidently with people and with their environment.

Self-Concept: In the early weeks a baby feels like an extension of his mother or primary caregiver. He doesn't really have a sense of self. However, as he becomes more alert, he begins to play with his hands and feet, interacts with others, and learns about separation from his caregivers.

 # How You Can Help

Approach and Withdrawal: Observe how your baby responds to bath time. Does he get excited, kick, splash, vocalize, and squeal? Or does he cry, squirm, and resist? Although both responses are considered innate, you can help make new situations easier for the resistant baby by talking to him, moving slowly to let him get used to things, and keeping the new experience short until he gets used to it.

Developing Trust: As your baby continues to learn to trust you, make sure you respond to his needs in a timely manner. The old adages "Let him cry it out" and "You'll spoil the baby if you pick him up too much" are outdated and may even be harmful. If your baby wants attention, give him attention. Pick him up, carry him around, and nurture him. He'll take this foundation of trust into adulthood and be a happier, more successful person.

Self-Concept: Continue to provide your baby with lots of mirror time to help develop his self-concept. He likes to look at people, but he's especially interested in his own image, and he'll make different faces and sounds at the reflection in the mirror.

Week 9: Curiosity

 ## Baby's Physical Development

Soft Spot: Your baby has two soft spots (fontanels) on her head, a larger one on the top and a smaller one at the back. By now the posterior (back) fontanel has probably closed, meaning the cartilage has hardened into bone. The other fontanel won't harden and close until your baby's about a year and a half old.

Scooting: Your baby may show signs of beginning to scoot while she's lying on her tummy. She'll raise her buttocks in the air and try to push off the carpet or floor. You may find that when you leave the room and return minutes later, she has miraculously inched across the floor.

Weight Gain: Your baby adds about a half pound around this time. Since your baby's digestive system is not ready for solids, since solids may cause her to develop allergies that could be avoided, most pediatricians recommend waiting to introduce solids until around six months. They also encourage parents to feed their babies primarily breast milk or formula throughout the first year.

 ## How You Can Help

Soft Spot: Your baby can develop a flat head if she spends too much time in one position, especially on her back. Since putting your baby to sleep on her back is now recommended to help prevent sudden infant death syndrome (SIDS), make sure to change your baby's position often while she's awake. Give her plenty of propped-up sitting time and time on her stomach.

Scooting: To encourage scooting, place your baby on her tummy on a soft surface. Place your open hands at the bottoms of her feet, to provide resistance, and gently push them forward. Your baby should tuck her legs and raise her buttocks. While she's in this position, keep your hands steady, and she may begin to shove herself forward.

Weight Gain: Your baby is digesting her food better and spitting up less. It's tempting to introduce cereal at this time, when you hear the old wives' tale about how it helps a baby sleep through the night. But this is a myth. Babies have their own internal clocks, and they'll sleep through the night when they're ready. Your baby won't need solids for several more months.

Baby's Cognitive Development

Brain Growth: Your baby's brain grows at an amazing rate during the first year. At birth her brain weighed about twenty-five percent of the adult weight. By the end of the first year, her brain will weigh about fifty percent of the adult weight, and will weigh seventy-five percent by age two.

Memory: Your baby's memory is developing each time she's reintroduced to a plaything, person, event, and so on. By now she can remember something that happened as long as a week ago, if the experience was exciting enough to captivate her attention the first time.

Language Development: Your baby is making new sounds and learning to play with her lips, tongue, and throat. She likes to coo and listen to the sound of her voice as she repeats noises. She also likes to gurgle the saliva at the back of her throat and make other interesting sounds.

 # How You Can Help

Brain Growth: As your baby's brain grows, it's important that you continue to stimulate her through language, experience, sensation, and so on. The more she's stimulated, the further and faster her cognitive abilities will develop. Play with her, talk to her, show her the world, and give her the opportunity to interact with playthings and people.

Memory: Select a toy that makes a noise when gently squeezed. Place it in your baby's hand, squeeze it for her, and watch her reaction. She'll soon be squeezing it herself in an attempt to make the noise. Her memory is developing, and she's learning about cause and effect.

Language Development: Coordinating the parts of the mouth for speech is tricky business—and lots of fun! Practice a variety of sounds with your baby while she sits facing you. Gurgle, blow bubbles, make raspberries, puff your mouth, whistle, make teeth noises, and so on. Be creative. She'll be fascinated, and soon she'll be making those sounds herself—great practice for various speech sounds.

Baby's Psychological Development

Adaptability: Some babies easily adapt to changes in their environment, schedule, and caregiver. Others become irritable if their routines are disturbed or interrupted. This aspect of personality seems to be innate.

Interaction with Environment: You may begin to see your baby interact more specifically with familiar toys or playthings. She's using her senses to explore the properties of objects, and she's learning about them through frequent contact.

Loneliness: Your baby feels lonely at times and may simply want to be picked up, held, and talked to. She'll let you know she wants attention by looking for you, calling out, fussing, or crying. Your close proximity makes her feel comforted, safe, and secure.

How You Can Help

Adaptability: If your baby seems happier with the same routine, you might try to keep it as consistent as possible. If you want to introduce change with such a baby, do it slowly. Talk to her about what's happening in a tone of voice that's reassuring and comforting, and try to keep changes to a minimum.

Interaction with Environment: When you offer your baby a rattle or soft toy to hold, watch how she interacts with it. She may look at it, shake it, squeeze it, put it in her mouth, even throw it—all to see what it's about. Show your baby how to manipulate her toys by demonstrating their properties. Then let her try them out with your help.

Loneliness: When your baby is feeling lonely, you might consider keeping her with you as you move around the house or apartment. A great way to do this is to wear her in a front pack, sling, or backpack. If you must leave her for a moment, talk to her while you're gone to let her know you're nearby. Even though she won't see you, she'll sense your presence and be comforted.

Week 10: Reaching

 ## Baby's Physical Development

Reaching: Your baby is practicing his reach by extending his arms and pulling them back again in an effort to make contact with objects he perceives. At the same time, he's kicking his legs to help propel his reach.

Grasping: Grasping is no longer primarily a reflex. When your baby makes contact with an object after reaching for it, he's probably grasping it tightly, waving it around, moving it into his field of vision, grasping it with his other hand, and trying to put it in his mouth.

Tonic Neck Reflex: While lying on his back, your baby has a tendency to turn his head to one side, keeping that arm and leg extended while flexing the opposite arm and leg, as in a fencing posture. He's getting used to the left and right sides of his body. He will soon turn his head without drawing up an arm and leg.

 ## How You Can Help

Reaching: As your baby thrusts his arms forward in an attempt to reach objects, offer him a chance to make that connection. Place him in an infant seat and hold a colorful plaything an inch or so from his reaching hand. Wiggle the object around, and watch him try to grab for it. Make sure he's successful!

Grasping: As your baby's ability to grasp objects increases, he needs lots of fun things to hold. Offer him a variety of toys that are easy to hold and let him explore each one. When he drops an object, offer him a different one. Then offer him an object while he's holding something else. See what he does!

Tonic Neck Reflex: After you change your baby's diaper, check his tonic neck reflex by gently turning his head to one side. Watch to see if he curls the opposite arm and leg. Gently turn his head to the other side, and see if he does the reverse. Show him a toy, and see if he turns his head to follow it.

Baby's Cognitive Development

Listening Skills: Your baby's listening skills are improving rapidly as he's becoming acquainted with different sounds in his environment. He may try to search for an object that makes a noise, or he may demonstrate recognition of a familiar sound by kicking his legs and vocalizing.

Depth Perception: The foundation of depth perception should be developing about this time. Your baby is still not able to understand how steps work or why a toy falls to the floor, but he blinks when you bring a toy too close to his face, and he startles when you suddenly lower him.

Vocalizing: Your baby will begin making new sounds now that he's learned how to manipulate his mouth and tongue. He loves the reaction he gets from parents, and he can entertain himself for some time with squeals, laughter, and fake coughs.

 ## How You Can Help

Listening Skills: Play a listening game with your baby to help enhance his ability to locate a sound. Find some interesting toys that make noises. Seat your baby in his infant seat or on your lap, then make a noise with one of the toys, just beyond his field of vision. Watch him try to turn his head and eyes to find the sound. Bring the object into his field of vision to help him make the connection between the toy and the noise.

Depth Perception: Find a colorful toy and hold it about twenty-four inches from your baby's face. As you slowly bring the toy closer, wiggle it and have it make noise to attract his attention. Notice the point at which he tries to reach for the toy, kicks his legs in anticipation, or blinks.

Vocalizing: Increase your baby's vocabulary by imitating the new sounds he makes. Add a few more and see if he copies them. To encourage his laughter, make funny faces, play Peek-a-Boo, and laugh with him. Don't tickle him, though; that's torture!

Baby's Psychological Development

Self-Awareness: Your baby always has playthings at the tips of his fingers: his fingers! He tends to play with them now each time he rediscovers them. He may watch them, clasp them together, wave them, and put them in his mouth to learn more about them.

Intensity of Reaction: Some babies really show their emotions. They giggle and laugh out loud when they're happy, or they scream and cry when they're sad or mad. Other babies are more reserved and don't show their feelings dramatically. These tendencies seem to be innate.

People Person: Your baby responds to human faces more than pictures or designs. He also recognizes when a normal face is missing a part (nose, eyes, mouth). His intense identification with your face enhances his attachment to you.

 # How You Can Help

Self-Awareness: Make finger play even more fun by putting a baby sock, with the toes cut out, on your baby's hand. Draw a funny face on the sock with a non-toxic felt-tip pen, and make sure the face is turned so he can see it. Watch what he does with his hands and the sock.

Intensity of Reaction: If your baby tends to really show his emotions, he may need more calming down when upset. If not calmed down, he may work himself into further distress by his reactions. Provide a calming atmosphere when he's gearing up, so he can better control himself.

People Person: Watch your baby's reaction to your face by showing him different expressions. For fun, create different faces by using a piece of Scotch tape. Place it across your nose, over your lips, down one eye—anywhere that changes your appearance. Show him your new face, and watch his reaction. Talk to him to reassure him it's still you, then remove the tape and watch his reaction.

Week 11: Self-Awareness

 ## Baby's Physical Development

Sitting Up: Your baby should be sitting well now with support. Her head is steady enough to stay erect for short periods of time, and she can move it from side to side in short bumpy jerks. Soon her head movements will be smooth and controlled.

Sleeping: About one-third of American babies sleep through the night at this age. Their days are becoming longer and more interesting, and their brains are maturing. Although some babies respond to parents' attempts to help them learn to sleep through the night, trying to make your baby fit into your schedule may cause more problems than necessary.

Fine Motor Skills: Your baby is better able to grasp and hold objects now, and she can bring them to her mouth. This takes considerable coordination and a release of reflexes. She's using her whole hand instead of her fingers, which will come later.

 ## How You Can Help

Sitting Up: When your baby sits up, make her world more interesting by placing her in front of exciting things to watch. Set her in her infant seat to watch you work, place her near the window so she can see the dog or kids in the yard, or turn on a TV show that's appropriate for young children and see if she shows any interest in the movements on the screen.

Sleeping: Parents can influence their baby's sleep patterns in different ways. For example, if a parent reacts too quickly to her baby's early morning cries, the baby is likely to continue this pattern. If a parent initially ignores those cries, the baby may go back to sleep and lengthen her sleep pattern. Instead of responding too quickly in the morning or in the middle of the night, give your baby a few minutes to calm herself and possibly go back to sleep.

Fine Motor Skills: Give your baby lots of easy-to-grasp objects and watch what she does with them. Place them near her while she's on her tummy, or wave them in front of her as she sits in her chair. Her grip isn't easily released, so practice by gently massaging her fingers until she lets go.

Baby's Cognitive Development

Depth Perception: Your baby is beginning to understand depth perception on a basic level. She can tell the difference between a continuous solid surface, like a floor, and one that drops off, like a stairway, but she can't process what will happen if she goes down the stairway. As she begins to crawl, she becomes even more aware of the difference through experience.

Distance Perception: Your baby can now see twice as far as when she was born. She's able to see and understand that when her parents are two or three feet away, they are still her parents, even though they look smaller.

Scanning: Your baby demonstrates a rudimentary scanning ability as early as three months. This skill develops over time, and it eventually enables her to learn to read. You'll see her eyes move from object to object, as long as the objects are within her field of vision.

 # How You Can Help

Depth Perception: To help develop your baby's depth perception, place her on a thick pillow on a floor near a short step. Place a toy near the edge of the step, and push it over the edge. Watch her reaction. Help her retrieve the toy by bringing her down to the toy's level.

Distance Perception: As your baby begins to recognize you from a distance of two or three feet (or more), talk to her and wave your hands to show her where you are. Then move closer, still chatting to keep her attention. Do the same with a large toy. Wave it, make noise with it, and move it closer to keep her focused.

Scanning: To help your baby practice scanning between two objects, hold up an interesting toy, then hold up another toy a few inches from the first. The toys should be positioned at roughly the same distance from her eyes. Watch her eyes to see what she looks at. Hold both toys steady, then wiggle one while keeping the other still. After she looks at the moving toy, stop moving it and wiggle the other toy. Watch her eyes scan to the newly moving object.

Baby's Psychological Development

Distractibility: At around three months babies begin to show levels of distractibility. Some babies are easily distracted from their interest or fussiness by a new toy, a song, and so on. Others cling to their interest or fussiness more single-mindedly.

Synchrony: Between two and three months babies begin to respond to their parents by smiling, chortling, kicking their legs, and opening their eyes wide. Parents and baby are becoming more synchronized as they read each other's eyes, body language, and facial expressions. This is the foundation for social interaction, and many parents "fall in love" with their babies during this time.

Emotional Range: In the early days your baby seemed to have only two emotions: frustration/distress, demonstrated by crying, and contentment, demonstrated by quiet behavior. As she fine-tunes her emotional expressions, she begins to show interest, curiosity, pleasure, excitement, sadness, and irritation.

 # How You Can Help

Distractibility: If your baby is easily distracted, there are tricks you can use to help her when she's fussy. Hold an attractive or new toy where she can see it. Move it around, make noise with it, or sing along with the movement. Sometimes a change of scenery will distract a fussy baby, so try taking her to a different room. At other times nothing but rocking will soothe and distract a fussy baby.

Synchrony: Share a little in-sync time with your baby by holding her in your lap facing you. Show her some facial expressions, do a few vocalizations, and watch her try to imitate you. Then watch her face for a while, and copy her facial expressions and sounds. You're having a conversation!

Emotional Range: As your baby shows more diverse emotional expressions, you learn to respond in appropriate ways. If you know she's sad or irritable, you can calm her more quickly. If she's happy or excited, you can join in her fun. If she's content, you can leave her to herself to enjoy her fingers, toys, or surroundings.

Week 12: Reaching Out

 ## Baby's Physical Development

Neck Control: Your baby can probably hold his head up for several seconds now, and he should demonstrate even better neck control in the next few weeks. He's eager to see the world from an upright position, and this encourages him to practice balancing his wobbly head.

Pre-Crawling: When you place your baby on the floor, he may make crawling movements such as flapping his arms and kicking his legs out like a frog. These actions don't do much to propel him forward, but he's practicing alternating the right and left sides of his body, a pre-crawling skill.

Eye Control: Until this time your baby has exhibited a doll's eye reflex, which means he opened his eyes each time you raised him to sitting as he was lying on his back with his eyes closed. This reflex should disappear now. His eye control is increasing, and he's opening and closing his eyes at will.

 ## How You Can Help

Neck Control: Help your baby improve his neck control by placing him in a propped-up position with a headrest. Bring a toy near his face to attract his attention, then pull it back gently. Watch him try to lift his head from the headrest to follow the toy. He may reach out with his hands, which will help move his head forward and will assist his balance.

Pre-Crawling: As your baby's swimming reflex disappears, he begins to make deliberate crawling movements. Help him practice this by placing him on his tummy. Sit behind him and alternately flex his legs. Watch his arms to see what happens. After a few minutes, alternately flex his arms and see what happens.

Eye Control: Check to see if your baby still has the doll's eye reflex by raising him to sitting while he's lying down with his eyes closed. If he does, lay him back on the floor, and talk to him to keep his interest. Continue talking to him as you raise him to sitting. He might maintain eye contact with you.

Baby's Cognitive Development

Increased Vocalization: Your baby is going to add even more sounds to his repertoire: ones he hears in his environment and ones he creates with his mouth. Listen for grunts, puffs, sighs, bubbles, squeals, and lots of vowel sounds. Vowels are easy to make since they only require an open mouth and a little sound. He may also smack his lips in anticipation of feeding time.

Voice Recognition: Your baby will probably look intently at the person speaking to him now, instead of looking around randomly. Words and voices really capture his attention. He's also beginning to tell familiar voices apart, such as dad versus siblings.

Color Preferences: Babies at this age begin to recognize more colors and may even show a preference for a particular color. Most babies like brighter colors (red and yellow) more than quieter colors (blue and green). Adults usually prefer the opposite.

 # How You Can Help

Increased Vocalization: Sing songs to your baby to increase his attention to vocal tone, tempo, and pitch. He especially likes higher sounds, so use your best soprano voice. Make up sounds occasionally. Your baby will watch you intently and perhaps try to sing along.

Voice Recognition: Play a guessing game with your baby. Ask another family member to join you, then seat your baby in his infant seat or prop him up so he can see both of you. Cover your mouths, and have one person speak. Watch your baby try to figure out who's speaking by making eye contact with the speaker.

Color Preferences: Check to see if your baby prefers a particular color by performing a simple test. Find four similar objects that are four different colors (red, yellow, blue, and green). Hold them up one at a time and watch your baby's face carefully. If his eyes light up or if he kicks his legs more for one color than for the others, he may prefer that color.

Baby's Psychological Development

Selective Smiling: Your baby will show a preference for certain people by reacting to them differently, often with a smile. If he smiles widely, he probably recognizes or likes the person. If he smiles slightly, he may not know the person well or may not feel as comfortable around the person. If he doesn't smile at all, he probably doesn't recognize—or like—the person.

Threshold of Responsiveness: Some babies are sensitive to noise, touch, and bright lights. They startle, wake up, or cry in response to a stimulus. Other babies seem to sleep through anything: sudden lights, loud noises, being moved, even wet diapers.

Comfort and Contact: Even though your baby is becoming more independent and alert, he still requires lots of holding, touching, cuddling, and nurturing. He'll soon be off exploring on his own, so use this time to give him plenty of physical affection.

 # How You Can Help

Selective Smiling: Watch how your baby reacts to new faces. Sometimes a stranger can elicit a smile just by smiling at your baby. At other times strangers can scare your baby with their unfamiliar faces. Slowly introduce a newcomer to your baby, and let him get used to the new face. After a few minutes have the person talk to your baby. See if he's more receptive to the stranger as he gets to know her or him.

Threshold of Responsiveness: Your baby's sensitivities are innate; there's not much you can do to change them. Be aware of your baby's responses, and try to accommodate them. If he's sensitive to his environment, try not to startle him. If he doesn't seem easily startled, you can relax more, but don't forget about him!

Comfort and Contact: Continue making time each day for physical comfort and contact with your baby. Infant massage is a wonderful way to do this. Pay special attention to his hands and fingers to encourage his awareness of his fine motor ability. You might also consider enrolling in a baby exercise class to share some physical time with other parents and babies.

Week 13: Vocalizing

 ## Baby's Physical Development

Pre-Standing: Your baby's legs are straightening out more as the weeks pass. She stretches her legs when held upright, and she tries to press her feet on flat surfaces. She may even make stepping movements when held upright in a standing position, something she used to do as a reflex.

Neck Strength: Your baby's neck is even stronger now. As a result, she's balancing her head so she can see more of the world. She still needs support when sitting for longer periods, but you may find her leaning forward in an attempt to control her head.

Arm Waving: Your baby's arm strength is also increasing. She likes to wave her arms simultaneously, flapping them up and down. She'll soon be able to control her arms, but now she's merely practicing movements.

 ## How You Can Help

Pre-Standing: Make sure your baby has bare feet and is wearing loose clothing or only a diaper, if it's warm enough. Lay her on her back, grasp her back and sides, and gently raise her to sitting. (Make sure her neck is strong enough to support her head.) Gently raise her to standing while keeping her feet near the floor. Watch to see if she presses her feet flat on the floor. With your continued support, let her balance on her legs. Check to see if she raises a foot.

Neck Strength: To increase your baby's neck strength, place her on her back and press against her feet with your body to keep her from sliding. Grasp her arms, and gently raise her to a sitting position. She should right her head as she reaches a vertical position.

Arm Waving: To help your baby increase her arm control, give her lots of opportunities to move and wave her arms. The best position for this is sitting or lying on her back. When she flaps her arms, imitate her movements, and watch her increase her waving and flapping. Then move one of her arms and see what she does with the other.

Baby's Cognitive Development

Scent Memory: Right from birth, one of your baby's best-developed senses is her sense of smell. She already recognizes her parents' scents, and now she's able to recognize other familiar smells such as baby lotion, certain fragrant toys, mom's perfume, and so on. Even milk has a scent she remembers.

Listening to Vocalizations: You baby loves the sound of her own voice. She's added many sounds to her repertoire, and she can probably entertain herself for several minutes just by vocalizing.

Circular Vision: Your baby's ability to track objects is expanding rapidly. She can look side to side, up and down, and in a small circle. As her visual skills increase, so does her interest in the world.

 # How You Can Help

Scent Memory: As your baby comes in contact with familiar scents, let her hold the items near her face so she can smell them. Say the names of the items, remove them from her face, then bring them back and let her smell them again. Let her smell a variety of items, and watch her reactions. You might try a lemon, a banana, some cheese, or other foods. Try to avoid bringing her near unpleasant smells.

Listening to Vocalizations: Tape-record your baby's vocalizations and add a few of your own to encourage new ones. Play the tape for her to enjoy and watch her listen attentively to her own voice.

Circular Vision: Try a game of Follow-the-Light. Sit in a darkened room with your baby in your lap or in her infant seat facing a wall. Shine a flashlight on the wall, and watch her attend to it. Move the light back and forth, up and down, and around in circles. Move it slowly so she can follow the image.

Baby's Psychological Development

Gestures with Vocalizations: As your baby increases her vocalizations, she begins to imitate your gestures by waving her arms and legs as you talk with her. This "conversation," using pre-speech and early gestures, is clearly a social interaction that takes place between babies and their caregivers. These conversations enhance your baby's cognitive skills and emotional attachment to her caregivers.

New Awareness of Caregiver: Babies at this age are especially attentive to their caregivers. You'll notice that your baby gets upset when you leave, gets excited when you enter the room, and follows you with her eyes when you move around.

Eye Contact: Your baby's eye contact with you is increasing. She can gaze at you for longer periods without needing a lot of attention-getters. This eye contact is more than just watching; it's an emotional connection that's important to the bonding process. Notice how she smiles, vocalizes, and moves her body more when making eye contact with you.

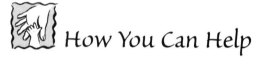 How You Can Help

Gestures with Vocalizations: This is a good time to play Pat-a-Cake. Seat your baby in her infant seat and sit opposite her so she can see you clearly. Play Pat-a-Cake with her. Go through the motions while holding her hands and chanting the song. Try it without holding her hands, then try it again while holding her hands. Soon she'll begin waving her hands in anticipation of the game.

New Awareness of Caregiver: Notice how your baby follows you around the room with her eyes. Play a game of Hide-and-Seek by ducking behind counters and chairs, then popping out to surprise her. Move around the room to keep her alert to the game and trying to anticipate your next move.

Eye Contact: As your baby meets your eyes, talk with her to maintain the connection as long as possible. To keep her interested, move your head slightly, widen your eyes, blink, and smile.

Week 14: Coordination

 ## Baby's Physical Development

Coordination: Your baby's arms and legs are beginning to move in a coordinated fashion. You'll see him kicking his legs alternately while he's on his tummy (a pre-crawling movement) and moving his arms simultaneously (a balancing activity). While he's standing with your support, his rubbery legs may bend under him (another pre-crawling exercise).

Head Lift: Your baby should now be able to lift his head while lying on his tummy. Make sure he's on a soft surface in case his head drops suddenly.

Finger Coordination: Your baby's grasp is well established by now, and he'll soon be opening and closing his fingers around an object rather than merely wrapping them tightly.

 ## How You Can Help

Coordination: While your baby is lying on his tummy kicking his legs, move his arms in alternating actions to simulate crawling. Also practice rotating each of his arms. While he's standing with your help, have another person lift one leg and then the other, to practice left and right sides of motion.

Head Lift: To help your baby practice head lifts, place him on his tummy. Set a toy in his field of vision, then move it upward to encourage him to lift his head and follow the toy with his eyes. Move it slowly and make noises with the toy to keep his interest.

Finger Coordination: Play finger games to help your baby open and close his tight grasp. Show him your open hands, then close them. Repeat this several times, occasionally wiggling your fingers as you open them. Then gently help your baby open and close his fingers. Sing, "Open them, shut them" as you play.

Baby's Cognitive Development

Cognitive Coordination: Until now your baby has been holding and looking at objects without really knowing that he has something in his hand. But now he's beginning to look at the object as he brings it to his mouth. His brain is beginning to coordinate the object he feels with the object he perceives in his hand.

Visual Convergence: As you bring an object into your baby's field of vision, he tries to focus on it. Although he may look cross-eyed, his depth perception is improving. He should be seeing fairly clearly when the object is one to three feet in front of his face.

Discrimination: Your baby may now interact with different toys in different ways, as he learns to distinguish the properties of the toys. For example, he may scratch one toy, mouth another, drop another disinterestedly, and just stare at another toy.

 How You Can Help

Cognitive Coordination: While your baby is holding an object, draw his visual attention to it by shaking it, tapping it, or pointing to it. If he's holding the object to his side, move his arm into his field of vision. Talk about the object and watch to see if he makes eye contact with it.

Visual Convergence: To help your baby focus both eyes on a nearby object, find a colorful toy and hold it a few feet from his face. Bring it closer, moving it slightly, and notice when he makes eye contact with it. Move the object closer until he stops looking at it. If he reaches for the object as it gets within his grasp, he's showing signs of increasing depth perception.

Discrimination: Check to see how your baby reacts to different objects. Offer him a rattle, and see if he brings it to his mouth. Offer him a fuzzy animal, and see if he holds or drops it. Offer him a piece of paper, and see if he tries to scratch it. Offer him a new toy he hasn't seen before, and see if he just stares at it.

Baby's Psychological Development

Quality of Mood: Some babies seem happy all the time. They smile, laugh, giggle, and are quiet. Every new sight, sound, or object seems to elicit joy or pleasure. Other babies seem irritable, fearful of meeting new people, unhappy with change, and fussy throughout the day.

Vocalization: Your baby is getting better at expressing his emotions by vocalizing instead of crying. For example, he may fuss when he's hungry, babble when he wakes up, and whine when he's wet. If you listen carefully to his cues, you'll be able to respond quickly and appropriately, encouraging the positive expressions while discouraging the negative ones. He still cries vigorously if he's hurt, scared, or seriously distressed.

Strange versus Familiar: As more people interact with your baby, he begins to display preferences toward some people. Notice his reactions toward different people and see if they remain consistent from visit to visit.

 # How You Can Help

Quality of Mood: Although experts believe babies are born with their temperaments, you can help alter your baby's moods to some degree. Role model a positive attitude by speaking in a calm voice, by smiling throughout the day, and by talking to your baby as you introduce new situations, activities, or playthings. Over time he may learn to overcome his darker moods and have a more pleasant outlook.

Vocalization: As your baby "talks" to you, mimic the vocalizations that are speechlike, but not the ones that are unrecognizable. This should help increase his awareness of important sounds, and he'll begin to make even finer vocal discriminations.

Strange versus Familiar: If your baby seems reluctant to be held by someone, encourage that person to talk softly to your baby, to approach him slowly, and to ask permission to pick him up by using a kind voice, a positive facial expression, and outstretched hands. If he allows the person to pick him up, have the person hold your baby in a gentle and relaxed way.

Week 15: Excitement

 Baby's Physical Development

Shoulder Lift: As your baby's neck grows stronger by the week, you see dramatic changes in her head lifts. While on her tummy, she may now be lifting her shoulders along with her head, enabling her to see more of her exciting world. This is another step toward crawling.

Standing Strong: Your baby's legs are getting stronger, and she's able to stand with support for longer periods. She likes to extend her legs and balance briefly with her feet on a flat surface. She'll soon be ready for an exersaucer that allows her to jump up and down with support.

Water Fun: Bath time turns to playtime for your baby about now, as she discovers the many properties of water. This wonderful environment stimulates your baby's senses, and she enjoys exploring its many possibilities.

 How You Can Help

Shoulder Lift: While your baby is lying on her tummy, move her arms out to her sides with her elbows bent and hands forward, to help her support her head and shoulders. Then lie down opposite her in the same position, so you're facing each other. Talk with her to encourage her to lift her shoulders.

Standing Strong: Give your baby lots of exercise to help strengthen her growing legs. Hold her around her waist with her feet on a flat surface, then relax your hold as she balances herself. Catch her if her rubbery legs start to collapse!

Water Fun: Make bath time fun time by providing toys, bubbles, and mild splashes as you gently scrub your baby clean. She enjoys sucking on a wet washcloth, watching bubbles pop, and reaching and grasping for toys that bob on the surface. She'll soon learn how to splash by herself, and she'll be surprised and delighted by the cause-and-effect response.

Baby's Cognitive Development

Anticipation: Watch for signs of anticipation in your baby as she begins to remember events, activities, and playthings she's experienced. If you make a particular sound when preparing to feed, change, bathe, or hand her a toy, her gestures and vocalizations will let you know she remembers.

Consonants: There should be new sounds coming from your baby's lips as she plays with her mouth, teeth, and tongue: consonants. As she brings her tongue back into her throat, you may hear "na-na," "ga-ga," and "ba-ba."

Visual Acuity: As your baby's visual clarity and distance perception improve, she's better able to focus on and follow smaller objects. Prior to this time she had difficulty spotting and tracking objects that weren't at least an inch wide or larger.

How You Can Help

Anticipation: As your baby learns to anticipate, you can begin to teach her how to transfer that anticipation to related situations and playthings. For example, you might shake a rattle behind your back, then show her another toy that's similar to the rattle. Watch her reaction as she tries to process the surprise.

Consonants: Help your baby practice consonants by first repeating her vocalizations, then adding a few of your own. If she says, "na-na," first repeat it, then say, "ta-ta" (the "t" sound involves a similar but slightly different tongue placement). For "ga-ga," try, "ka-ka," and for "ba-ba," say, "pa-pa." These other sounds are more challenging for her to vocalize, but they are the next step in speech development.

Visual Acuity: Now that your baby can track items that are less than an inch wide, try a little experiment. First show her a large item, then move it around so she can follow it with her eyes. Replace it with a smaller item, and repeat the movement. Repeat using smaller and smaller items, and watch your baby track them.

Baby's Psychological Development

Attention Span: While some babies attend to an activity or toy for a relatively long time, others lose interest quickly and want a change. This behavioral tendency is largely innate, but attention span can be lengthened to some degree with practice.

Mirror Fun: Your baby enjoys looking in the mirror as she grows and changes. She may even smile at herself, pat herself, and get excited when she sees her reflection.

Daddy Play: Child development experts have noticed that Daddy Play is different from Mommy Play, and that babies respond differently to various styles. Your baby is hearty enough to enjoy the more vigorous play usually provided by dad, such as holding her up high, swinging her from side to side in his arms, and "flying" her on his knees. But when she gets hurt, she usually wants mommy's comfort.

 # How You Can Help

Attention Span: To help your baby increase her ability to attend, spend one-on-one time with her by entertaining her with a special toy, song, or book. If she starts to get fussy, see if you can extend the playtime a minute or two by using a different tone of voice, by moving the object around, or by adding something to the play. TV is another way to increase a child's attention span, as long as the program is fast moving, colorful, and interesting.

Mirror Fun: Place your baby in her infant seat close to a mirror, so she can enjoy her image. Then look at her in the mirror, talk to her, and see if she can figure out where you really are (inside the mirror or right next to her). Make faces and show her how to entertain herself with funny faces.

Daddy Play: Mom, you can do this, too! Simply swing, fly, or lift your baby around in the air. She may giggle and laugh out loud during this type of play, something she may not do during quieter activities.

Week 16: Babbling

 ## Baby's Physical Development

Weight Gain: By this time your baby has doubled his birth weight—an amazing rate of growth second only to his rate of growth in the uterus. Much of the early weight is fat, which provides insulation and stores nutrients.

Night Sleeping: About one third of American babies are sleeping through the night by the third or fourth month. "Through the night" is defined as six hours at a time. The other babies continue to wake up sometime during the night because they're hungry, wet, or needing attention.

Grasping: Your baby continues to practice his reaching-out skills, and he will try to grab objects in front of him. Sometimes his timing is off; he grabs too soon or too late. When he does make contact, he can lose interest quickly and let go. He especially loves to grab your hair, so watch out!

 ## How You Can Help

Weight Gain: Your doctor will be checking your baby's weight gain, but you can usually tell if he's healthy just by looking at him. A few babies seem to want more than milk at this time, and the introduction of rice cereal is fine. Most pediatricians don't recommend solid foods until around six months, but every baby is unique. Some will be hungry for solids sooner. Just make sure you don't replace milk with cereal.

Night Sleeping: Sleep cycles can be affected by parents' caregiving patterns as well as by baby's maturity. A baby becomes conditioned to waking up, so parents might consider letting their baby determine his schedule to some extent. Parents can help regularize and lengthen their baby's sleeping patterns by putting him down at a regular time, by letting him comfort himself for a short time during the night, and by making sure he gets regular naps.

Grasping: Help your baby practice grasping more accurately by waving an object slowly in front of his hands, making sure it's within his reach. If he grabs too quickly or too slowly, time your movements to fit his speed as you repeat the action. Make sure the items are easy to grasp.

Baby's Cognitive Development

Object Permanence: Babies at around four months show early signs of learning that an object still exists even if it's moved out of sight. They demonstrate this recognition with wide eyes, still bodies, extra sucking, and sudden movements. In a few more weeks your baby will not only know an object still exists, he'll begin searching for it.

Conversation: Your baby's vocalizations may change around this time as he begins to listen more to other people's speech. He may grow quiet when you talk and he may make sounds when you stop talking. He's learning how to vocalize, listen, and wait for a response. This is the foundation for conversation.

Judging Distance: Your baby will blink when something moves too close to his face, something he wasn't doing much before now. This indicates that he's beginning to learn more about distance and when objects are coming closer to his eyes.

 How You Can Help

Object Permanence: Playing Peek-a-Boo helps your baby understand the concept of object permanence. By making your face disappear for a few seconds, your baby learns that you haven't vanished forever. To enhance the game, put a cloth over your face, talk to your baby, then lean in toward him. He may grab the cloth off your face. Watch him light up when he finds you!

Conversation: Practice having a chat with your baby by saying something short and simple. Then pause and let him have a chance to "talk." Repeat what he says, then add a few more sounds, words, or vocalizations. Keep taking turns as long as he remains interested.

Judging Distance: To check your baby's blinking ability, bring a toy close to his face from a distance. Notice when he blinks. To help him practice judging distance, seat him in his highchair at a table. From the other side of the table, roll a ball toward him. Watch him follow the ball with his eyes and see if he blinks as the ball approaches.

Baby's Psychological Development

Emotional Expression: Your baby is probably laughing more now, especially during play. While dads tend to make babies laugh more than moms do, dads also tend to make babies cry more, at which point babies tend to prefer mom's comfort. Babies are also beginning to show anger at this time, when they become frustrated or restricted from moving.

Crying: The old wives' tale about letting a baby "cry it out" is no longer respected by today's child development experts. Letting a baby cry does not help expand his lungs or keep him from becoming spoiled. Furthermore, it does not diminish the crying, and it can lead to a withdrawal of emotional expression over time, as a baby learns that he gets no response when he cries.

Social Being: As your baby becomes more of a social being, he probably prefers being around other people over being alone. He may show this through fussing, demanding attention, wanting to be held, and crying when he's alone.

 How You Can Help

Emotional Expression: To encourage your baby's laughter, make playtime more exciting with surprises, large movements, tummy bubbles, and Gonna-Get-You! To minimize his feelings of anger, try to determine and eliminate the cause if possible. Your baby is beginning to understand that he's a person, and these are the first signs of his growing independence.

Crying: Instead of ignoring your baby's cries, respond to them. This teaches him that you are there for him, that you care, and that he's not alone. Pick him up, carry him around, distract him with a toy, change his scenery, or simply hold him until he's calm. Crying is his only way of communicating his fears, loneliness, discomfort, and anxiety.

Social Being: Try to keep your baby with you when he's awake. He enjoys your company and will be more content if he sees you nearby. Invite a child to play with him from time to time—babies love children! Be sure to keep an eye on them, especially if the older child doesn't always know how to properly interact with a baby.

Week 17: Oral Exploration

 ## Baby's Physical Development

Sitting Propped: Your baby is sitting better while propped up, and she's enjoying watching her world. She can sit longer without toppling because her back is less rounded. Her lower back area is still curved, but it's beginning to straighten out, which will soon allow for more overall body movement.

Two-Hand Grasp: When you give your baby a toy, she tends to grasp it with both hands. She may release one hand temporarily, but she probably regrasps the object with both hands after a short time. Then she likely brings the toy to her mouth to check it out.

Wrist Rotation: About this time your baby is beginning to rotate her wrist while holding a toy. This allows her to examine more angles and properties of the object. She'll have this down in another three to four months.

 ## How You Can Help

Sitting Propped: Your baby enjoys being pulled to a sitting position when she's lying on her back. As she's lying down, let her grasp your thumbs or fingers (you'll feel the strength of her grip). Then slowly pull her to a sitting position.

Two-Hand Grasp: Practice the one-hand grasp with your baby, which is the next step in deliberate grasping. Hand her a toy near the center of her body, and watch what she does. Then hand her a toy closer to one hand than the other. She should take the toy in one hand, but she'll probably grasp it with the other hand as well. Then give her another toy from the side, and see if she releases one hand to grasp it.

Wrist Rotation: To help your baby practice wrist rotation, play a game of Bye-Bye. Seat her in your lap facing you, then wave to her while saying, "Bye-bye." Raise her arm and mimic the gesture with her hand. Play a few times, then repeat the game later to see if she moves her hand up and down.

Baby's Cognitive Development

Fine Motor Skills: Your baby is enjoying her fingers more and more. She's beginning to understand how they work and what they can do. Manual dexterity is important for all kinds of tasks, so give her opportunities for finger play by placing her in a sitting position so she can see and use her fingers.

Syllables: As your baby's language skills develop, she's beginning to string together specific speech sounds she hears from you. She's practicing her syllables, another part of the foundation for making words and sentences.

Location of Sound: Your baby's listening skills are improving. She's distinguishing more and more sounds, and she's recognizing the ones that are repeated and familiar to her. She's also trying to locate sounds that may not be in her field of vision. Now that she has better head control, she may be turning her head to find the sound, instead of using only her eyes.

 # How You Can Help

Fine Motor Skills: Although your baby enjoys playing with her fingers and can entertain herself for some time by wiggling, clasping, and sucking on them, you can enhance her manual dexterity with finger plays. Begin with simple games such as Open-Them-Shut-Them, Five-Little-Monkeys, and Where-Is-Thumbkin? As you sing each song, move her fingers to match the lines.

Syllables: Singing to your baby is one of the best ways to encourage her ability to vocalize in syllables. Using a simple tune as a foundation, sing strings of syllables using the sounds she makes or "la-la-la." Let her watch your face and mouth as you sing. She may try to imitate the song.

Location of Sound: Find two objects that make very different sounds. Place your baby in her infant seat with the objects out of sight, one on either side of her. Manipulate one object to make a sound, and see if she tries to locate it. Repeat with the other object. She may follow your hand to lead her to the object, so keep your hands out of sight (sit behind her, if necessary). See if she tries to turn her head in addition to using her eyes to locate the object.

Baby's Psychological Development

Special Attachment: Your baby may become attached to a special toy, blanket, or pacifier at this time, so watch carefully to see her reactions to different objects. She may light up when she sees her favorite toy, then frown if she sees something new. She's forming an attachment to something other than her parents, which helps her cope with her loneliness, fears, and insecurities.

Self-Calming: When your baby gets upset, she may try to calm herself by sucking her thumb or fingers or by putting her fist in her mouth. This is the first step in developing self-control and learning how to cope with emotional discomfort.

Emotional Expression: Your baby will begin to express herself more and more through play. When she shakes a toy or bangs it on the floor or table, she may be sharing her joy, frustration, anger, or excitement.

 How You Can Help

Special Attachment: When you notice that your baby is growing fond of a particular object, make sure it's available to her when she needs it. Attaching to a toy, blanket, or other lovey is a normal part of emotional development. It is not a sign of weakness. You can make her a special blanket for this purpose and keep it with her when she sleeps, travels, or needs extra comfort.

Self-Calming: When your baby begins to fuss, you might let her fuss for a few minutes to see if she can comfort herself with her hands and fingers. You can also provide her with a pacifier. Keep it handy so she can get it when she needs it. You can tie the pacifier to a very short ribbon (not too long or she could get tangled), and pin the ribbon to the front of her outfit. Do NOT turn the pacifier into a necklace; she could strangle on the ribbon. You can also have lots of pacifiers handy in case she drops or loses one.

Emotional Expression: If your baby likes to bang her toys but is driving you crazy, you can muffle the racket by putting a cloth on the table, by letting her bang in carpeted areas, or by giving her softer toys to express her feelings. Or get earplugs!

Week 18: Movement

 ## Baby's Physical Development

Lifting Up: As your baby's head, neck, and shoulders become stronger, he may lift his chest from the floor to about ninety degrees. This "seal" lift gives your baby an even better view of his world, and it leads to the next step in development: creeping.

Thumb Grasp: As your baby's grasping skills improve, he may begin to include his thumb instead of just his four fingers. This demonstrates a big change in his ability to handle objects.

Holding a Cup: Your baby may now be able to hold a plastic cup with two hands and lift it to his mouth. This will eventually lead to his ability to drink from a cup and feed himself—major developmental milestones.

 ## How You Can Help

Lifting Up: Lay your baby on the floor with his arms facing forward. Get down on the floor opposite him, and place a toy in front of him just out of his reach. Move the toy around to attract his attention, and see if he reaches for it. Then raise the toy up and watch him raise his chest off the floor in an attempt to follow it.

Thumb Grasp: To develop your baby's awareness of his different digits, play with his fingers and wiggle his thumbs. When handing him a toy, brush it against his thumb first, then slip it into his hand. If he grasps the toy only with his four fingers, uncurl his thumb and slip it around the object.

Holding a Cup: While your baby is sitting in his infant seat, give him a plastic cup to hold. The best kind is one with handles on both sides, as this allows him to grasp with both hands. While he's in the bathtub, dunk the cup into the water and watch what he does with it.

Baby's Cognitive Development

Eye-Hand Coordination: When your baby reaches for an object, he's using his hands while watching with his eyes. The entire movement is coordinated by his brain, which helps him determine how big an object is, how far away it is, and whether he can grasp it. As his eye-hand coordination develops, your baby will be able to do more complicated tasks such as drawing and writing.

Cause and Effect: As your baby's brain develops, he begins to figure out simple cause-and-effect tasks that lead to higher cognitive skills. He's already learned that when he cries, someone comes to get him. When he sucks at the breast or bottle, milk comes.

Attention Span: Your baby's interest in people and objects around him is growing and helping him increase his attention span. He's most interested in objects that engage many of his senses: objects that move, make noise, have a texture, produce a smell, tickle his tongue, are bright, and so on. He plays with objects that interest him longer than ones that don't.

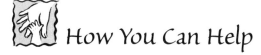 # How You Can Help

Eye-Hand Coordination: Place your baby in his highchair and set a toy on his tray or on a table nearby. Move the toy and watch his eyes follow the object. Move it out of sight and see if he continues to look for it. Bring the toy back to the table and set it close to him. If he grasps it, place another toy on the table in a different spot. Repeat this activity to see if he locates the toy when it's in a different location.

Cause and Effect: Place your baby in his infant seat. Tie a large ribbon (about a foot long) to a favorite toy. Tape the other end of the ribbon to a tray or table placed nearby. Set the toy on the tray, making sure the ribbon cannot be wrapped around his neck. Let him pick up the toy and play with it. Eventually he will drop the toy. When it falls from the tray, show him how to grasp the ribbon and pull the toy up. He'll soon learn this exciting skill, which also enhances his understanding of object permanence.

Attention Span: You can help your baby increase his attention span by playing with him and by keeping the games and activities exciting. When he shows signs of waning interest, move the object around, show him new properties, and think of new ways to talk about the object.

Baby's Psychological Development

Mirror Play: Your baby continues to be fascinated with his image, even though he's still not quite sure it's him on the other side of that mirror. He begins to understand cause and effect as he moves his arms and legs—and his image does the same. Mirror play is great visual stimulation for your baby, and it should be reintroduced each week to enhance his development.

In Sync: Your baby not only has "conversations" with you by exchanging vocalizations and taking turns making sounds, he also moves his body in rhythm with your speech. He seems to anticipate when you are going to speak next, how long you will speak, and when it's his turn to talk. You and your baby are becoming "in sync."

Recognizing Faces: Your baby prefers real people to toys, and he distinguishes faces from other patterns. He can recognize differences between familiar faces, and he reacts strongly to a face that frightens him. He may even react negatively to you if you make a face that disturbs him, such as crying.

 # How You Can Help

Mirror Play: Each time your baby interacts with a mirror, he learns something new. At first he was visually stimulated, but now he's beginning to recognize the person in the mirror. Join your baby during mirror play by sitting next to him, talking to him, and pointing to the mirror to show him your image. Then make a funny face in the mirror and watch his reaction.

In Sync: Watch your baby as you speak to him, and see if he moves in anticipation of your speech. Then pause for a moment before speaking again and see what he does. Is he reading your facial expression or sensing your patterns? Change your movements and patterns to find out.

Recognizing Faces: Since your baby loves faces, now's a great time to begin puppet play. Buy or make a puppet that has a simple, clear, brightly colored, well-defined face. Use the puppet to talk to your baby, tickle him gently, sing to him, and generally entertain him. You should get big laughs during puppet play.

Week 19: Rolling

 ## Baby's Physical Development

Rolling Over: Any day now your baby may roll from her back to her stomach. She'll push one leg over the other, tuck her lower arm in, and propel herself the rest of the way over. Be sure to watch her carefully whenever she's on raised surfaces, since she may roll unexpectedly at any time. Rolling over is a major milestone.

Solid Food: Some babies will be ready for solids about this time, but most pediatricians recommend holding off for another month or two—or longer if your baby is not interested. Solids may cause allergic reactions, spit-ups, or tummy aches if introduced too soon.

Holding a Bottle: Your baby may have the manual dexterity to hold her own bottle around this age. Her two-handed grasp is fairly secure, and her awareness of the bottle is apparent. She may drop it several times, but her growing independence is a fair trade-off for the attempt.

 ## How You Can Help

Rolling Over: Let your baby have plenty of time lying on the floor on her back with no obstructions nearby. Place a toy on each side of her, just out of reach, so she'll be encouraged to try to grasp the toys, which could cause her to roll over.

Solid Food: If your baby shows signs of wanting a taste of your food, you can let her try a small bite as long as it's bland, soft, and not something she can choke on. Anything the size of a peanut is a hazard. Babies choke most commonly on nuts, popcorn, hot dog pieces, too much food in the mouth (such as a wad of mushy crackers), and sticky foods (such as peanut butter). Introduce only one food a time, and wait a week or so before trying the next. Never put solid food in a bottle—only formula or expressed breast milk. Your baby is not ready for cow's milk yet, either, until she's at least a year old.

Holding a Bottle: If your baby seems to want control of her food, let her have it. Fill the bottle only half full (to make it lighter), and use a bottle that keeps air from getting in. Some bottles are shaped so they're easier to handle. But don't give up your nurturing time completely. She still needs lots of cuddling.

Baby's Cognitive Development

Vowels and Consonants: Your baby's chatter increases as she expands her babbling vocabulary. She's having fun with mouth noises and syllables, going back and forth between vowels and consonants. Listen for repetition of syllables and wordlike sounds.

Visual Scanning: Your baby has better depth perception and much improved vision, and she can scan a room to locate a voice, toy, or moving object that interests her. This is preparation for reading at a very basic level.

Transferring Hands: As your baby continues to examine objects held in her hands, she may show the first signs of transferring a toy from one hand to the other. This activity is part of her exploration of an object and an early step toward learning to compare.

 # How You Can Help

Vowels and Consonants: Play a regular game of mouth noises, expanding your repertoire each time you interact. She loves hearing you squeal, growl, gurgle, blow bubbles, make raspberries, click your tongue, squeak your cheeks, and whistle. Watch her try to imitate some of the sounds that you repeat.

Visual Scanning: To help improve your baby's visual scanning ability, show her a large, colorful toy up close. Let her touch it, hold it, taste it, and examine it for a few minutes. Then gently take the toy from her, keeping it in her sight, and walk across the room. Place the toy where she can see it, then return to her side, blocking her view of the toy. When you reach her, ask her where the toy is, and gesture toward it. Watch to see if she scans for it and makes eye contact.

Transferring Hands: To encourage your baby to transfer objects from one hand to the other, approach her from one side and give her an interesting toy. She'll probably grasp the toy and hold it with both hands. Try putting your finger in one of her hands, to keep it occupied, before giving her the toy. See what happens.

Baby's Psychological Development

Self-Soothing: Your baby is continuing to calm herself by using a number of handy and convenient techniques. This ability to soothe herself emotionally helps her cope with stress. You might see her sucking her thumb more often, rubbing her hair or head, caressing her blanket, or holding tightly to a lovey.

Emotional Distress: When your baby is really upset, the best form of comfort you can offer is physical contact (holding and rocking her). She may not calm immediately, but your presence and attention are already giving her comfort.

Facial Expression: Your facial expression, body language, and overall demeanor can greatly influence your baby's moods. She responds quickly and positively to smiling or laughing faces, pleasant moods, and relaxed body language. On the other hand, if you are angry or upset, your baby will sense this and may respond in kind.

 # How You Can Help

Self-Soothing: Although you want to come to your baby's aid when she needs you, self-soothing can help her learn to take care of herself. The pacifier is a good tool for this, so be sure she gets plenty of sucking time. It's a great substitute for the parent when the baby needs emotional comforting. But don't let your baby do all her own comforting—she needs you.

Emotional Distress: There are techniques you can use to help soothe an upset baby. Vigorous rocking sometimes calms a crying baby, but don't be too vigorous. Wearing your baby in a backpack or front pack can also calm her. Sometimes white noise can help, such as a vacuum cleaner, clothes dryer, or repetitive music. The infant swing is often soothing, and many parents take their babies for car rides to calm them.

Facial Expression: Try to be pleasant around your baby even when you don't feel up to it. She doesn't understand your moods, and they may cause more distress to her than you realize. Raised voices, crying, and even long periods of silence can often affect your baby's mood, both short-term and long-term.

Week 20: Sitting

 ## Baby's Physical Development

Sitting: Your baby's back is stronger and straighter, and he's better able to sit for longer periods with a little support on his lower back. He may even sit for a few seconds unassisted. You may feel his back muscles tense as he tries to maintain his balance in the sitting position.

Pre-Creeping: Your baby is gaining muscle strength and coordination in his arms and legs, and he uses the surface he's lying on to move himself. Soon he'll be using his arms or legs (or both) to inch forward on his tummy. He may push himself backward before he goes forward.

Voluntary Grasp: By five months your baby is grasping objects voluntarily. It's no longer a reflex. He also keeps reaching for a toy until he makes contact. He enjoys the object he holds and is better able to manipulate it with his fingers.

 ## How You Can Help

Sitting: To help your baby practice sitting, hold him in your lap (facing away from you) and carefully release your support. Be ready to use your hands for support when he needs it. You can also prop him on the floor with pillows on three sides to see if he can support himself for a few seconds.

Pre-Creeping: Sometimes when a parent leaves the room for a few minutes, she's surprised to find her baby has moved from his original spot on the floor. This pre-creeping activity requires nothing more than space on the floor and an opportunity to practice. You can enhance this skill by setting a toy several inches in front of your baby to inspire him to move.

Voluntary Grasp: Your baby will enjoy sitting in his highchair with an array of toys on his tray. He can choose the object he wants to play with, then explore it until he drops it, throws it, or tires of it. Attach the toys to ribbons taped to the tray, so he can retrieve them when they disappear over the side. Make sure none of the ribbons can get wrapped around his neck.

Baby's Cognitive Development

Classification Skills: Experts have found that babies at five months are capable of classifying objects on the basis of shape, color, size, and number (up to three). This may indicate that the ability to sort things into categories is innate.

Parentese: Babies naturally prefer simple language rather than complex words and sentences. Parentese enables babies to learn more easily how to talk. They also prefer to listen to singing, expressive speech, and responsive conversation. When a parent uses questions, simple commands, and repetition, a baby is more apt to listen, differentiate the sounds, and respond.

Anticipation: Your baby loves to do things again and again. He learns from repetition and gets excited when he anticipates something he's familiar with. To enhance this learning process, the event must be repeated within a few seconds to be successful.

 How You Can Help

Classification Skills: Your baby can improve his ability to perceive differences between objects with a little help from you. Place him in his infant seat and show him two similar but different objects such as a round and square block, a large and small stuffed toy, and a red and green ball. Present each pair one item at a time and let him interact with it for a few minutes. Then offer him the other item. Place both toys side by side and let him compare their properties.

Parentese: You can help your baby make rapid gains in receptive language (understanding speech) by using Parentese. This means talking to your baby in a higher pitched and animated voice, keeping your vocabulary concrete and simple, using short repetitive sentences, and talking a lot with your baby.

Anticipation: Play repetition games with your baby, and watch him delight in anticipating your actions and the toys you use. Show him a toy, make it disappear for a few seconds, then make it reappear. Repeat the action until he grows tired of the fun.

Baby's Psychological Development

Emotional Expression: Your baby can associate emotional meanings with particular expressions (smiles, frowns) and tones of voice (encouraging, discouraging). He responds to these differences and uses them to help him express his own feelings appropriately.

Temperament: Experts have found that your baby's temperament is established by the time he's a couple of months old. By five months you may be able to tell which of the three basic types he belongs to. Forty percent of babies are considered to have an easy temperament, fifteen percent are slow to warm up, ten percent are difficult, and thirty-five percent are still not clearly defined.

Social Interaction: Your baby responds to others in a variety of ways. He vocalizes, squeals, laughs, waves his arms and legs, smiles, coos, and watches the other person. These are signs that he is attached to someone special—you!

 # How You Can Help

Emotional Expression: Make funny faces with your baby and use silly voices to match. Place him in your lap or infant seat facing you and see if he tries to imitate you. He may laugh, frown, or even cry if the faces are too disturbing. Watch his reaction so he doesn't become scared.

Temperament: If your baby is easy, he goes along with new experiences, smiles a good part of the time, and is easy to comfort. If your baby is slow to warm up, he might be shy, initially unwilling to participate in new experiences, and might need more encouragement (not pushing) than easy babies. If your baby is difficult, he's probably irregular in his moods, intense in his reactions, and difficult to calm. This baby may be a handful, and you may need extra support, more breaks from the stress of coping, and various techniques for calming him.

Social Interaction: Spend time each day interacting with your baby. Lie down on the floor and play with toys, chat while he's in his infant seat, delight him with games of surprise, and so on. The more time you spend with him, the better and more securely attached he will be.

Week 21: Socializing

 Baby's Physical Development

Mouthing: At this age your baby is probably putting everything she can grasp into her mouth. While lying on her tummy, she may reach for items around her and take them into her mouth to find out what they feel like, what size and temperature they are, if they're soft or hard, and even if they're edible. It's the way she learns about the properties of different objects.

Rollover: Your baby will soon be rolling over both ways if she isn't already. This is another major milestone, one that leads to greater mobility. Some babies use rolling over to get from one spot to another. Be sure to keep an eye on her at all times when she's on a raised surface.

Sitting: Sitting without support is another physical task your baby is trying to perfect as she attempts to hold up her head and straighten her back. She may even roll up into a sitting position, but she may tip over soon after.

 How You Can Help

Mouthing: Now that your baby's taking everything into her mouth, you need to be especially careful of her surroundings. She tries to mouth even the tiniest objects including coins, bits of food, and bugs. She could choke on these things, so make sure the area is cleared of objects that are sharp or breakable or have small parts. However, don't stop her from mouthing objects; it's still a valuable learning experience. Set out a variety of items for her to grasp and safely mouth while lying on her tummy.

Rollover: To help your baby practice rolling over, give her a little help by tucking in one of her arms and lifting the opposite leg over the other leg. She'll soon get the idea if she hasn't already. Place toys on either side of her and give her praise to keep her motivated. (The experience will do that, too.)

Sitting: Hold your baby in your lap and support her lightly around her waist. Release her for a few seconds and let her balance herself. After a few times repeat the exercise on the floor, spotting her with your hands as she tries to balance herself.

Baby's Cognitive Development

Self-Esteem: Your baby shows early signs of self-esteem when she wants a favorite toy, attaches to a lovey, or smiles at herself in the mirror. These behaviors are not selfish acts. They express her growing awareness that she matters.

Matching Sounds: Around this time your baby will begin to notice differences between similar sounds, and she will anticipate which object makes which sound. She's fine-tuning her listening skills and using sounds to help her identify different objects.

Social Language: Your baby is using syllables, vowels, and consonants to practice "social language." She's imitating the sounds she hears from the people around her, which is a form of pre-language. You're likely to hear consonants including "ba," "da," "ga," "la," "ma," "na," "pa," "ta," and "wa." The rest of the consonants are more difficult and will come later.

 # How You Can Help

Self-Esteem: One of the best ways to help your baby enhance her self-esteem is to give her lots of mirror time. At this age she may respond to a mirror by smiling at herself. Let her see herself standing up, sitting, and up close. Put a hat on her head and watch her react to her new image.

Matching Sounds: Play a listening game with your baby, using two toys that make similar but different sounds, such as two rattles. Hold up one rattle and shake it for her, then hold up the other and shake it. Repeat this a few times, and watch your baby's eyes go back and forth as she anticipates which will make the next noise.

Social Language: To continue your baby's rapid development of speech sounds, use songs or chants to repeat the sounds she makes. When she says a sound, imitate it, then make another sound that's similar. See if she imitates you. Say a few simple words that use similar sounds, and show her the objects that correspond to those sounds. For example, say, "dada" (point to daddy), "mama" (point to mommy), "baba" (point to a bottle), "wawa" (point to water), and so on.

Baby's Psychological Development

Social Interaction: Your baby is recognizing and responding to familiar people more and more. She watches people she's attached to, smiles at them spontaneously, vocalizes excitedly, and waves her arms and legs.

Social Play: Your baby is beginning to anticipate the fun of playing with you. She may be wide-eyed at first, but she'll eventually begin to smile and laugh and become excited. She may also begin to "ask" for the play to continue by making noises, waving excitedly, and fussing when it ends.

Emotional Expression: A few weeks ago, when your baby was upset, she tended to be comforted by rocking, swinging, or other physical methods. Now she tends to be comforted by being with the people she's attached to, by having her lovey, or by soothing herself with a pacifier.

 # How You Can Help

Social Interaction: Your baby becomes more comfortable with people as she spends more time with them. If she doesn't respond positively to a friend or relative, she probably needs time to warm up and get to know them. Have the person approach her slowly, talk to her, and continue to make attempts throughout the meeting. Don't force the friendship. Your baby will warm up when she feels comfortable with the person.

Social Play: Your baby will enjoy playing more games around this age as she learns how to interact with and respond to her caregivers. Continue playing Peek-a-Boo, Pat-a-Cake, Gonna-Get-You, and finger plays for fine motor development; Airplane for gross motor development; and Where-Did-It-Go? for cognitive development. All interactive play enhances social development.

Emotional Expression: Observe how your baby responds to your comforting methods. You may notice that different techniques work for different discomforts. Holding her, talking to her, and caressing her will often be enough to soothe her at this age. Sometimes a change of caregiver is needed if your baby continues to be upset. This gives both you and your baby a break.

Week 22: Responsiveness

 Baby's Physical Development

Pushups: When placed on the floor, your baby has the strength and coordination to push himself up with his arms. He can also lift his head, shoulders, and upper chest. Next he'll be lifting his tummy and progressing toward his legs and feet. Babies develop physically from head to toe (cephalo-caudal development) and from center to extremities (proximo-distal development).

Reach Around: Your baby's reaching ability has changed dramatically. He can reach up or down, straight ahead, to the side, and toward something that's moving around his body. He can grasp with one hand, transfer the object to his other hand, and hold a second object in the first hand.

Palmar Grasp: Your baby's grasp is becoming more coordinated and specific. He's beginning to learn to use his fingers individually. The palmar grasp should be evident by now, which means he's picking up objects with his third and fourth fingers rather than with all his fingers. Next he'll be using his thumb.

 How You Can Help

Pushups: You can challenge your baby to do pushups in a couple of ways. First, place him on his tummy on the floor, and put a picture under the top of his chest. Encourage him by doing a pushup while facing him. When he pushes up, he reveals the picture underneath his chest. You can also dangle a toy in front of his face and lift it slightly to encourage him to push up.

Reach Around: Play a game of Reach Around. Tie a toy to a short ribbon and hold the toy in front of your baby so he can grasp it. Move it up and let him grasp it, hold it down low and let him grasp it, hold it to the side and see if he reaches for it, and circle it around him to see if he anticipates and reaches for it.

Palmar Grasp: As your baby begins to grasp with the side of his hand and last two fingers, he's more adept at picking things up. To further develop this skill, offer him a variety of objects to grasp, such as a small ball, stick, cracker, and piece of paper.

Baby's Cognitive Development

Object Permanence: Your baby's cognitive skills are developing rapidly. He's learning that some things disappear but can be found again. He should begin looking for dropped toys around this time, if only for a few seconds. He'll soon search more persistently until he finds the object that has disappeared.

Face Recognition: Your face is probably the object your baby recognizes most easily. He sees it a lot, has a natural affinity for it, and is stimulated by it. You'll know by his response (wide eyes, open mouth, rapid sucking on his pacifier, or kicking legs) when he's noticed that part of a familiar face is missing or covered.

Water Play: Bath time should be lots of fun as your baby enjoys the sensation of water. While he's touching, splashing, and tasting the water, he begins to notice how different toys and objects behave differently in the water.

 # How You Can Help

Object Permanence: Continue playing Hide-and-Seek with your baby to increase his ability to search for missing items. Set a toy in front of him and make sure he sees it. Then cover it with a small blanket or washcloth. See if he notices the object is gone and tries to uncover it. Reveal the toy to him, if necessary, and play again until he gets the idea or grows tired of the game.

Face Recognition: You can play the Face Game a couple of ways. While sitting and facing your baby, cover one part of your face (eye, nose, or mouth) with your hand. If you're close enough to your baby, he might grasp your hand and try to move it away. You can also play the game with pictures of faces. Cover one part of a face with paper and see how he responds.

Water Play: Make bath time fun time and learning time by placing different objects and toys in the water. Give him soft waterproof toys, such as rubber ducks, and hard toys, such as small wooden boats, so he can examine them in the water. Add toys that sink and ones that float, and keep the water shallow so he can explore the differences in these properties. Add toys that pour, sift, fill, and squirt, such as measuring cups, colanders, plastic bottles, and turkey basters.

Baby's Psychological Development

Vigorous Play: Play stimulates your baby's physical, cognitive, emotional, social, and psychological growth. Social play helps your baby learn to interact with others in different ways, since everyone plays differently. Your baby also learns about his abilities, which in turn enhances his self-esteem. Vigorous play provides an emotional outlet, so you'll probably hear laughter when you engage in this type of play.

Object Response: Give your baby a new toy that's appropriate for his developmental level. He should respond to it in a number of ways. He may try to shake it, bang it, bite it, suck on it, stuff it in his mouth, and throw it.

Imitation: Speech sounds are not the only behaviors your baby will try to imitate. He's already copied some of your facial expressions, and he may now try to imitate your arm and hand movements or the actions of kids playing nearby.

 # How You Can Help

Vigorous Play: Play fun games with your baby that involve full body movement. Place him on his tummy on a blanket and drag him around the room for a Blanket Ride. Lie on your back and lift him on your bent knees for a Knee Ride. Lift him up and down for a Jack-in-the-Box game. Don't overdo the roughhousing, though. Your baby's neck is still somewhat fragile, so don't shake him, bounce him, or swing him too vigorously.

Object Response: Find a toy that encourages your baby to respond in several ways. A more complicated rattle, a musical toy, a soft doll, a squeaky toy, a Koosh ball, or a small pillow can offer your baby the opportunity to explore various properties.

Imitation: As you've done with facial expressions and vocalizations, repeat your baby's movements and actions to reinforce them. You can show him other behaviors, such as waving bye-bye, clapping, or opening and closing your hands, and see if he tries to copy you. Repeat the action several times, and manipulate his hands and arms to teach him the new movements.

Week 23: Creeping

 ## Baby's Physical Development

Creeping: The difference between creeping and crawling is all in the tummy. Your baby's first forward movements are most likely to occur any day now in the form of creeping (pushing or dragging herself a few inches across the floor). At this stage babies tend to move in a froglike manner, with most of the action in the arms and legs.

Sitting with Support: Your baby is making great strides in sitting with support. She may need only a small cushion to support her back. She's able to hold her head steadier, keep her back muscles tenser, and balance herself far better than only a few weeks ago.

Tactile Stimulation: Your baby's tactile awareness is becoming more sophisticated. She can tell when a cloth is wet or dry, a new toy is hard or soft, an object is rough or smooth, or your hands are warm or cold. She's learning about her environment through her hands and her sense of touch.

 ## How You Can Help

Creeping: To encourage your baby to creep, lay her on her tummy on the floor and place your hands against the bottoms of her feet. As she curls her legs, keep your hands against her feet. When she straightens her legs, she'll propel herself forward using your hands for leverage. Set a toy in front of her as a goal.

Sitting with Support: Since your baby is eager to see the world in an upright position, give her time to practice sitting with support. Place her on the floor in a sitting position with cushions or other back support behind her to help her maintain her balance. Give her a toy to hold, and watch her react to her new position as she shakes the toy and challenges her balance.

Tactile Stimulation: Here's a fun game to increase your baby's tactile awareness. Collect pairs of objects that are rough and smooth, warm and cold, soft and hard, and so on. Give her one from a pair to touch, then give her the other. Watch her expression as she notices the differences. Use the appropriate words to describe the sensations she's experiencing. For fun, put a little jam on her fingers and let her feel the stickiness.

Baby's Cognitive Development

Cause and Effect: Your baby is increasing her cognitive skills as her brain weight reaches fifty percent of the average adult. She's continuing to absorb information through her senses and build on that information. For example, when she shakes a rattle, the result is motion and sound. She repeats the action, increasing the motion and sound. Soon she'll repeat the action with a different toy, exploring cause and effect to see if the second toy moves the same way and makes the same sound.

Memory: Your baby now remembers objects or experiences that occurred a couple of days ago. Some experts claim that babies retain memories for up to two weeks. Parents often say their babies can remember even longer than that.

Pitch and Tone of Voice: Your baby has probably been vocalizing for several weeks now, making noises, vowels, consonants, and even the occasional word-like sound. Now she begins to modify the pitch and tone of her voice to make it sound like yours.

 # How You Can Help

Cause and Effect: As your baby builds on her ability to cause something to happen, to experience the effect, and to learn the relationship between the two, give her ample opportunities to develop this important skill. Offer her objects that produce an effect, such as a wet sponge (squeeze it and water comes out), a squeaky toy (squeeze it and it makes a sound), and playdough (squeeze it and it retains its new shape).

Memory: Play a memory game with your baby to increase her ability to recall. Give her a new toy and let her play with it for a while. When she's tired of it, put it away for a couple of days. Bring it out again and see if she plays with it the same way (from memory). Put the toy away, bring it out a week later, and watch her reaction.

Pitch and Tone of Voice: Practice speech sounds with your baby using songs, chants, and poems. Make your voice go up and down, then loud and soft, to attract her attention and make the words more interesting. See if she imitates you.

Baby's Psychological Development

Pleasure: Your baby experiences pleasure in several ways: through feeding, playing with a special toy, holding a lovey, being held by you, and so on. She hasn't often expressed her pleasure noticeably, but any day now she may start smiling when she's pleased. She's moving beyond the responsive social smile to smiling when's she's happy.

Anticipation: Watch your baby's body language (kicking her legs, flapping her hands, bouncing her body, and shaking her head) as you go through the day. As she begins to anticipate the routines in her daily life, she may let you know when she's ready to be picked up, fed, changed, and played with.

Awareness: As your baby grows increasingly aware of herself and her surroundings, she focuses more on her playthings. A few weeks ago she may have held or shaken a toy, but she probably didn't look at it much. Now she may study it as she holds it, experiencing it in a new way.

 # How You Can Help

Pleasure: Watch how your baby enjoys a toy by noticing her body language, vocalizations, and facial expressions. If you see a hint of a smile when she's enjoying herself, show her your smile, too. Social referencing can now be used to confirm how she feels rather than to tell her how you feel. Talk about her feelings, even though you don't think she can understand the words. She soon will.

Anticipation: Play a game that encourages your baby's anticipation. Find a toy that has a surprise element, such as Jack-in-the-Box or a pop-up toy or book. Prepare her for the surprise by talking in a monotone voice, then produce the surprise and show her your delight. Repeat the action and watch her reaction as she begins to anticipate what is about to happen.

Awareness: Now that your baby is more focused on objects themselves, give her playthings that have interesting and complex properties. Toys that make sounds, light up, offer detail, and can be manipulated are more attractive now. She's learning more as she handles and studies them.

Week 24: Tasting

 Baby's Physical Development

Gross Motor Skills: A few months ago, when your baby moved his arms and hands, he mostly flapped them, waved them without control, and focused more on the person holding the toy than the toy itself. Now that your baby is almost six months old, his arm movements are smoother, more controlled, and his hands can close around the toy as he focuses on it.

Creeping Faster: Your baby will continue to belly-crawl around the floor, once he's realized this form of locomotion gets him from place to place. He may also move around by scooting on his butt, by rolling over, or by pushing his feet off the floor. Watch his movements become smoother in the next few weeks as he prepares to crawl without dragging his tummy.

Tasting: Many babies are ready to taste their first solid food at around six months. At this time babies have less risk of developing allergies, spitting up, and rejecting the food. However, your baby still needs primarily breast milk or formula during the first year.

 How You Can Help

Gross Motor Skills: Your baby has better control of reaching, grasping, manipulating, anticipating, and coordinating his movements into a smooth organized action. Help him practice this remarkable achievement by playing Can-You-Get-It? Hold a toy within his reach, and slowly move it around. He'll soon reach for it and eventually grasp it.

Creeping Faster: Make sure your baby has a smooth, comfortable surface on which to explore his surroundings. If the floor is rough, scratchy, cold, or uneven, he may be reluctant to practice crawling. If he's not quite ready to try it, get on your tummy and show him how it's done.

Tasting: Since breast milk provides iron, vitamin C, antibodies, digestible fats and sugars, hormones, and other growth factors, it's the best food for your baby. Nevertheless, doctors recommend introducing solid foods at six months of age to get babies used to the taste. Start with simple rice cereal, since it provides iron and vitamins, is easy to digest, and doesn't have a strong flavor.

Baby's Cognitive Development

Intermodal Perception: This is a time of big changes in your baby's cognitive skills. At around six months your baby is able to associate information from one sense with that from another. He can determine people's moods, discriminate between genders, and even match speech sounds to the right lips.

Sensorimotor Intelligence: Your baby learns a lot about his surroundings through his senses, which in turn stimulate a motor response. Nearly everything in his world causes a response: lights, sounds, tastes, touches, and so on. This perception-and-action learning is immediate, and it leads to the understanding of concepts.

Babbling: Your baby's noises are becoming more varied as he practices his speech sounds. By six months he may repeat favorite syllables in a sentence-like stream such as "da-da-da-da-da." He likes playing with his mouth, tongue, teeth, and vocal chords.

 # How You Can Help

Intermodal Perception: As your baby's brain begins to coordinate information from his senses, offer him playthings that stimulate all his senses. Food is one of the common ways a baby improves his intermodal perception. If you give your baby a banana, he can see it, smell it, touch it, squeeze it, and taste it. But the best intermodal plaything is YOU.

Sensorimotor Intelligence: Since your baby gathers most of his information through sensory perception and motor response, play games that produce this kind of reaction. Turn on a light, and watch him try to locate it with his eyes. Make a sound, and watch him turn to it. Touch his palm with a toy, and watch him grasp and explore it. Open a jar of peanut butter under his nose, and watch his motor response!

Babbling: If you listen carefully, your baby may make certain sounds in certain situations, as if he's applying "words" to specific people, objects, or experiences. For example, you might hear "da-da-da-da" when dad is around. However, he might use the same expression for mom, a sibling, or even a stranger. He'll fine-tune his vocalizations over time as he hears words repeated.

Baby's Psychological Development

Social Referencing: At six months your baby will deliberately search his caregivers' faces for emotional information. If a situation is new or causes anxiety in your baby, he will look to his parent for reassurance. Babies also notice a difference between mothers, who tend to be more protective, and fathers, who tend to be more encouraging.

Attachment: Your baby shows attachment for his parents and caregivers by freely exploring new toys, by missing his caregiver when she or he is gone, and by getting excited when his caregiver returns. The more he feels attached, the more he tends to venture out, knowing he's safely connected to his loved ones.

Social Gestures: Although your baby doesn't use specific words to express his needs, he's beginning to use more gestures to let his caregivers know what he wants. For example, he reaches out his arms to be picked up, he holds on tightly to remain with his caregiver, he arches his back to be put down, and so on.

 # How You Can Help

Social Referencing: You can influence your baby's responses to ambiguous situations by simply changing your facial expressions. Use this ability to help him ease into an uncomfortable experience, try a new food, or explore a new toy. Soon he'll be checking your face on a regular basis to see whether a situation is safe, fun, or frightening.

Attachment: Encourage a secure attachment in your baby by being sensitive to his needs, by responding to his signals, and by playing with him to encourage his growth and development. The more he attaches to you now, the more independent he'll be in the future.

Social Gestures: Respond to your baby's gestures so he knows you're listening and you understand. As you read his gestures, use the words that describe his desired action. For example, if he's smiling and kicking his legs, say, "You're so happy!" If he's reaching for something, say, "Do you want that toy?" He's using mostly body language now, but as he listens and receives language input, he'll eventually learn the appropriate words.

Week 25: Wondering

 ## Baby's Physical Development

Teething: Teeth may appear any time between four and twelve months, most commonly between six and eight months. You'll notice your baby beginning to drool, but the appearance of teeth will probably take some time. She may be fussy just before a tooth breaks through, and she'll probably suck, rub her gums on firm objects, and bite to relieve the irritation.

Standing: Your baby's ability to stand continues to improve rapidly. She should be able to support most of her weight for a few moments, although her balance is still shaky. If she's still a little bowlegged, it's perfectly all right for her to practice standing. Bowlegs used to be related mainly to poor health and rickets, but we now know that some babies' legs are more bowed than others due to position in the uterus. They will outgrow this in time.

Seal Pushups: Your baby continues to practice "seal" pushups, using her arms to raise herself off the floor. As her arms become stronger, she gets better at dragging herself across the floor, which eventually leads to crawling.

 ## How You Can Help

Teething: Help your baby get through teething periods by providing lots of cold, smooth, firm objects for her to suck and chew. You can also rub your finger across her gums occasionally, but be prepared—she may bite down. If she bites during breastfeeding, just pull back, let her know it hurts by frowning and saying, "Ouch!" and let her try again. She's capable of learning that when she bites, she doesn't get milk for a few seconds.

Standing: Let your baby practice standing to help develop her leg muscles and balance. While she's in a sitting position, let her grasp your thumbs, then gently pull her upright. Let her feel her balance for a few seconds. When she feels more secure, see if you can withdraw one of your thumbs. If she's not ready to let go, don't force it.

Seal Pushups: Hold a toy in front of your baby to increase her desire to raise herself up. Then set the toy a few inches away from her to encourage her to go after it.

Baby's Cognitive Development

Imitation: Your baby continues to imitate your speech sounds and gestures more accurately, so listen closely for her ability to recreate what she sees and hears. It's a major milestone and another building block for cognitive learning and language development.

Wondering: As your baby explores her environment, her curiosity grows. She can turn her head and search for sounds, look for toys that have disappeared, and begin to move toward a desired object. Every encounter with her environment provides a learning opportunity.

Baby-Proofing: As your baby becomes increasingly mobile, it's time to baby-proof your home. Babies surprise us by getting into dangerous situations before we realize it, so prepare your home and make sure her learning environment is safe.

 # How You Can Help

Imitation: Play Copy Me games with your baby, to give her a chance to practice more sounds and gestures. Pat-a-Cake and Peek-a-Boo are still solid options, but now you can add simple songs and finger plays to expand her repertoire, such as Hickory-Dickory-Dock, Whoops Johnny, Head-Shoulders-Knees-and-Toes, and Round-and-Round-the-Mountain. Basic sign language introduced at this age also helps babies increase their receptive and expressive language skills.

Wondering: Encourage your baby's interest in her environment. Create interesting sounds for her to locate and hide colorful objects for her to uncover. Expose her to various things she can see, feel, hear, touch, and smell. Field trips are great at this age, so take her to the zoo, park, museum, aquarium, lake, and so on.

Baby-Proofing: To make sure your home is safe, lock up cleaning items and poisons, secure drawers and cupboards with baby locks, gate stairs and off-limits rooms, put away sharp objects and small objects she can swallow, remove poisonous plants, and make sure doors and windows have safety locks.

Baby's Psychological Development

Likes and Dislikes: Watch your baby for clues about what she likes and dislikes. She probably uses facial expressions, body language, and sounds to communicate her delight with a person, object, or experience, or to indicate distress, irritation, or unhappiness with something or someone.

Moods: Your baby may go from happy to sad, from peaceful to mad, and from excited to fearful in a matter of seconds. Fast and frequent mood swings are normal for your baby at this age. They will grow less extreme and more stable over time.

Name Recognition: Your baby's name is important to her, and she needs to hear it often to learn that it belongs to her. A name that's difficult to say can be shortened or simplified. (She may do that on her own when she begins to speak.) There's no need to correct her mistakes or mispronunciations; she'll eventually do that on her own.

 # How You Can Help

Likes and Dislikes: When your baby shows emotions regarding things such as a toy, bath, or taste, say the words that describe her feelings. This will help her accurately describe her emotions when she acquires language. She's absorbing vocabulary and learning through repetition within the context of experience, so give her lots of input. She'll soon be expressing herself with words.

Moods: Help your baby learn to temper her moods by distracting her from her fears and irritations. Play with her, show her a new toy, change her environment, and so on. You're not denying her feelings; you're giving her a chance to calm down and return to more positive emotions.

Name Recognition: Besides using your baby's name frequently, play the Name Game with her. Sing the song, "Baby, baby, bo-baby, banana-fana fo faby, me-my-mo-maby, baby!" or make up your own version. Show her pictures of other people when you sing their names, then point to your baby when you sing her name. Play Peek-a-Boo by covering your baby's head, then asking, "Where's (baby's name)?" Pull off the cloth and say, "There's (baby's name)!"

Week 26: Understanding

 Baby's Physical Development

Raking: In the past few weeks, you've been helping your baby relax his tight fist to an open palm. He now begins to vary his grip, using his hand and fingers in different ways. He may begin to rake the ground as he attempts to pick things up. He's learning a more effective way of getting what he wants.

Weight Gain: Your baby has doubled his weight by this time, primarily by taking in breast milk or formula. The average weight for a six-month-old is between sixteen and eighteen pounds, but this varies. As long as your baby looks healthy and is gaining weight, he probably weighs what's right for him.

Height: Your baby gains weight rapidly during the first six months, but he's a little slower to grow in height. Most babies are eighteen to twenty-two inches long when they're born. The average is twenty inches. At six months he's probably twenty-five to twenty-six inches long. Surprisingly, he'll reach half his adult height by two years of age!

 How You Can Help

Raking: You can help your baby practice raking with his fingers. Put little stickers on the backs of his fingers, or make dots with a non-toxic felt-tip pen, to help him pay attention to his fingers. Place a toy on the floor in front of him as he lies on his tummy. He should reach and grasp the toy using an open-finger grip, unless he's too distracted by the decorations on his fingers!

Weight Gain: If your baby is off the charts on weight gain, you don't need to put him on a diet. He just needs to move a little more. Begin a program of moderate exercise, using a baby exercise book as a guide. If he's underweight, you might increase his feedings or give him a little more solid food to satisfy his appetite. Check with your pediatrician to make sure he doesn't have any medical problems related to his weight.

Height: There's no need to worry about your baby if he's on the short side. He's genetically programmed to grow to a certain height, and as long as he receives good nutrition, he'll reach his full potential. Feed him well and schedule regular checkups with his doctor.

Baby's Cognitive Development

Fine-Tuning: Your baby is becoming more and more fascinated with the details of objects as his vision improves, his brain grows, and his world provides more to look at and explore. He's enjoying more complex toys at this age than he did in earlier weeks.

Searching: Your baby has a pretty good handle on object permanence at six months. When you take away an object he shouldn't be holding, he may protest, try to reach for it, and even go in search of it if he's mobile.

Rhythm: Babies begin to get a feeling for rhythm in speech, in play, even in routine. You may hear him try to imitate the rhythm of your conversations. He may want you to repeat a particular game. He's even learning to repeat his actions to create rhythm, as in clapping.

 # How You Can Help

Fine-Tuning: Give your baby the opportunity to explore toys that offer more interesting details, such as toys with patterns or faces, toys with lots of colors, toys with a variety of textures, or toys that make different sounds. Show him the toy, let him explore it, then show him the many properties of the toy so he can expand his interaction with it.

Searching: If your baby gets hold of something dangerous, replace it with something he can play with, instead of just taking it away. This redirection to a new object will likely cause him to forget the forbidden object. Whenever possible, remove dangerous or forbidden objects before he gets hold of them.

Rhythm: Play a song and clap to the rhythm. Encourage your baby to clap, too, even if he can't quite keep up with the beat. He's beginning to understand repeated patterns, and clapping is a way to help him control his rhythms.

Baby's Psychological Development

Stranger Anxiety: Babies have definite preferences about who they like and don't like, and they may show stranger anxiety when an unfamiliar person approaches. They may pull away, hold the caregiver tightly, fuss, scream, or cry. This is a normal reaction. Your baby is getting better at recognizing the differences between people, and he naturally prefers those he's familiar with.

Playful: The more you play games with your baby, the more he understands how the games work, and the more he expresses his emotions during play. He may anticipate the actions of a game, and he may even instigate a favorite game such as Peek-a-Boo.

Voice Recognition: Babies at this age are capable of recognizing familiar voices. When your baby hears someone he knows, he may smile, vocalize, kick his legs, flap his arms, or try to move in the direction of the speaker.

 # How You Can Help

Stranger Anxiety: Don't push strangers on your baby. Let him warm up slowly on his own. Simply explain to the person that your baby is experiencing the normal stage of stranger anxiety, and that he may soon come around. Try to avoid the words *shy* and *afraid*. Babies at this age don't usually like Santa Claus or Halloween costumes either, so don't force these things on your baby until he's ready.

Playful: Look for signs that your baby wants to play. Offer him some of the props you use when you play, and see if he begins the game. You might place a cloth in his lap for Peek-a-Boo, or give him a ball to throw for Baby-Throw-and-Catch. He also shows interest in play by gesturing that he wants the play repeated or by fussing when the play ends.

Voice Recognition: Play a game with your baby to see how well he recognizes familiar voices. Place your baby in his infant seat and have familiar family members and friends talk to him from behind. Watch his different reactions to the voices. Have the speaker reveal himself or herself to your baby and see if his reaction changes.

Week 27: Identifying

 ## Baby's Physical Development

Pincer Grasp: Your baby is practicing a new grasp called the pincer grasp about this time. She's using her thumb and forefinger to pick up objects, without using her palm. This is a big step in the development of fine motor skills.

Head Control: Your baby's neck muscles should be quite strong now. She should be leading with her head as she's pulled to sitting. Her head should no longer be lagging as it did a few weeks ago. If she's not leading with her head, check with your pediatrician.

Stronger Stance: Your baby should be balancing on her legs for longer periods now. She stiffens her legs and bears the weight of her body in an attempt to remain standing.

 ## How You Can Help

Pincer Grasp: Now that your baby can pick up objects with her thumb and forefinger, small items such as beads, coins, and marbles become even more dangerous. Make sure you remove these choking hazards from her play areas. You can still provide her with pincer-grasp practice by placing frozen peas on her highchair for her to pick up and eat. Frozen peas can also help soothe a teething baby.

Head Control: To help your baby strengthen her neck and lead with her head, do some baby pull-ups with her. Gently pull her up to sitting from a lying down position. She should anticipate each pull-up by tightening her neck and raising her head.

Stronger Stance: Place your baby in a standing position, and have her hold onto your thumbs. Release one thumb, let her maintain her balance, then release your other thumb. Keep your hands near her body in case she relaxes or loses her balance.

Baby's Cognitive Development

Two Syllables: As your baby continues to produce pre-speech sounds, she begins to repeat syllables. You may think she's trying to say words, but she's usually just practicing her vocalizations. Pre-speech is not only fun for your baby, it helps her better control her utterances.

Receptive Language: Your baby can recognize the words you say most often, especially if they refer to concrete things and actions, such as "dog" and "bye-bye." When you say these familiar words, watch for signs of attention from your baby, including eye contact, wide eyes, and raised eyebrows.

Improved Vision: Between the ages of five and seven months, your baby's vision improves to the point where she can more clearly see objects smaller than an inch wide. This leads to more attention to detail, better focusing, and improved eye-hand coordination.

 # How You Can Help

Two Syllables: When you hear your baby repeat syllables, imitate them back to her. Then make up new two-syllable sounds for her to imitate. The most popular sounds at this time are "da-da," "ba-ba," "ma-ma," and "ga-ga." Try to expand her sounds to include more difficult consonants such as "ka-ka," "la-la," "pa-pa," "na-na," and "fa-fa," but don't expect her to pick them up quickly.

Receptive Language: When you say simple words to your baby, try to show her something concrete or active to go with them so she can make the connection. For example, when you say "bottle," point to a bottle. When you say "bye-bye," wave good-bye. Repeat the words several times in a high-pitched voice, and keep the sentences simple.

Improved Vision: Gather several small objects less than an inch wide, and move them around in your baby's field of vision. Watch her follow the objects with her eyes and perhaps try to reach for them. If she grasps an object, make sure it doesn't go into her mouth. Place frozen peas on her highchair tray so she can eat them after she grasps them.

Baby's Psychological Development

Attachment: As your baby grows increasingly secure in her attachment to you, she begins to show the same kind of affection, interest, and attachment to other members of the family and other caregivers.

Sick?: Your baby develops an interesting sound about this time—the fake cough! It's a great way for her to get attention, and it's fun to make. You may hear other strange noises including growls, gurgles, snorts, and ear-piercing squeals.

Mirror Fun: Your baby really enjoys seeing herself in the mirror and watching her reactions. She may point to her body parts, try to touch her image, and distinguish between her reflection and yours.

 # How You Can Help

Attachment: Make sure other family members spend time with your baby as often as possible. She can get to know them better, enjoy their different interactions and personalities, and learn to feel safe with them. You might have a special game she plays only with a sibling, a different one for grandma, another one for grandpa, and so on.

Sick?: You can usually tell the fake cough from the real one. Listen carefully to the sounds, and make sure your baby isn't showing other signs of illness. If you're sure it's the fake cough, imitate it back to her, then enjoy a good laugh. Give her other silly sounds to try, such as simple animal noises.

Mirror Fun: As your baby looks in the mirror, point out what she's looking at. Begin with, "There's (baby's name)!" Then show her her nose, mouth, eyes, and ears. Then move her arms, legs, head, and tummy. Peek in and out of the mirror yourself, and call attention to your image when it appears. Put a hat on her head or cover her face with a cloth and watch her reaction.

Week 28: Problem Solving

 ## Baby's Physical Development

Holding: Your baby is getting better at holding a cup, and he may even manage to get some of the liquid into his mouth. He can grasp the cup with two hands, understand that there's something good inside, and figure out how to get it. He accomplishes this through observation, problem solving, cause and effect, and practice.

Chewing and Biting: If you haven't felt your baby bite down yet, try putting your fingers in his mouth, but be careful! At this age biting may be related to teething, but it may also be a new mouth game. He's also practicing chewing (or gumming if he has no teeth).

Nutrition: Your baby is probably trying more solid foods now, particularly fruits and vegetables. Milk is still the most important food for him, but supplemental solids will begin to provide more nourishment. Introduce one food at a time to see if he's allergic to it, and wait a week or so before trying the next one.

 ## How You Can Help

Holding: Give your baby a two-handled cup to hold as he practices this new skill. A covered cup or sippy cup helps prevent spills. Pour a small amount of liquid into the cup to prevent him from gagging and spilling too much on himself. Give him plastic cups and stacking cups to practice with in the bathtub.

Chewing and Biting: Give your baby both soft and firm foods to bite and chew, such as teething biscuits, frozen peas, banana bites, and baby crackers and cookies. Also provide him with teething toys and other safe objects to bite and chew. Make sure there are no parts that can come loose and present a choking hazard.

Nutrition: Parents often wonder whether to introduce fruits or vegetables first, after their baby has managed cereal. Experts are divided. Some say it's better to start vegetables first, because the baby is less likely to eat them if he tastes fruits. Others say fruits should happen first, because the baby will get used to solids more easily with the sweet taste. It doesn't really matter. You may choose to alternate between fruits and vegetables from week to week.

Baby's Cognitive Development

Dominant Hand: You may begin to notice your baby's hand preference even at this early age. Most babies are right-handed, fifteen percent are left-handed, and a few are truly ambidextrous (able to use both hands equally well). The dominance will become obvious as your baby acquires more fine motor skills.

Space: Your baby is getting better at perceiving depth and understanding spatial relationships. He'll be fine-tuning this skill in the next few weeks, but the three-dimensional world is becoming clearer to him.

Hand Transfer: Your baby is probably reaching and grasping with one hand now rather than two. Soon he'll be holding an object with one hand, then he'll be moving it to the other hand automatically.

 # How You Can Help

Dominant Hand: To find out if your baby is left- or right-handed, try this simple test. Give him a toy by presenting it to him midway between his hands. Watch which hand he uses to grasp the toy. Repeat the test several times. Avoid making hasty conclusions, though, because only time will tell what his preference will be. Also, don't try to influence his preference. Leave that up to him.

Space: To help your baby better understand dimensions of space, provide him with a variety of toys that stimulate this awareness, including blocks and empty boxes, balls and bowls, tubes and ropes, and so on. Play a fun game by placing him in a big cardboard box with the top open. Duck down and say, "Where's (baby's name)?" Then pop up to reveal yourself.

Hand Transfer: Place a toy within your baby's reach and watch him pick it up. Notice if he uses one hand or two. Then place another toy within his reach and see if he transfers the first toy, continues to hold it, or drops it. Hand him two toys at once, and see what he does with them. While he has a toy in each hand, offer him a third and see what happens.

Baby's Psychological Development

Social Referencing: As your baby grows more sensitive to his environment and the people around him, he continues to use cues from his caregivers to understand what's happening in ambiguous situations. He watches your face for emotional expressions, and he imitates you when he's not sure what's going on.

Play: Now that your baby has reached the second half of his first year, he's learning many important developmental skills through play. As he interacts with people and objects, he learns social skills, problem-solving skills, and physical skills. The first stage of play is called solitary play, in which he explores and manipulates objects on his own. This is followed by parallel play and cooperative play, which involve interaction with others.

Conversation: Your baby's language skills are increasing, and he's learning more about the social aspects of conversation. He may try to "talk" when you're talking (especially when you're trying to have a conversation with someone), but he'll gradually learn to take turns.

 # How You Can Help

Social Referencing: To help your baby cope with his emotions, use appropriate emotional expressions for him to imitate. If you're calm when a situation might be scary for him, he's more apt to remain calm. If you get upset, he'll probably get upset, too. Use social referencing to help him try new experiences.

Play: Since play is so important to your baby's development, spend at least half an hour twice a day interacting with him in a fun way. You might play social games such as finger plays, cognitive games such as Where-Did-It-Go?, and physical games such as Pick-It-Up or Flying Airplane. You'll find lots of good ideas in my book *Baby Play and Learn*.

Conversation: Give your baby the opportunity to imitate conversation. Say something to him, then pause to give him a chance to "say" something back. To keep the game interesting, change your tone of voice, make silly sounds and mouth noises, and use real words that he hears frequently. See if he begins to take turns "talking."

Week 29: Crawling

 ## Baby's Physical Development

Crawling: Around this time your baby is able to pull her tummy off the ground and crawl on all fours. Once she gets the hang of it, there will be no stopping her. When she reaches this stage, she'll quickly progress to other gross motor skills including standing and sitting alone.

Sitting Erect: Your baby is making rapid gains in all areas of body strength and movement. She may now be able to sit erect without support for a few moments. She may lean forward, place her hands on the floor in front of her, and support herself with her arms and hands. This is another major milestone.

Standing: Another major milestone is your baby's ability to stand alone for a few seconds. She's gaining leg strength from kicking, creeping, and standing practice, and she should now be able to stand erect and balance herself for a few seconds.

 ## How You Can Help

Crawling: Once crawling begins, a whole new world of fun and games opens up to your baby (and you). I'm-Gonna-Get-You! becomes more exciting, and now you can play Grab-and-Pull. Each time she gets up on her knees and crawls a few spaces, gently pull her legs out from under her and pull her back. This strengthens her legs by giving her more practice getting to all fours.

Sitting Erect: If your baby needs practice sitting up straight, you can help by placing her in a sitting position with her legs tucked criss-cross style or with one leg in front and one behind her, depending on her preference. Lean her over slightly, and place her hands on the floor. Place a toy on the floor in front of her. When she reaches for the toy, she may sit erect for a few seconds.

Standing: Give your baby lots of opportunities to practice standing. Hold her upright with her bare feet on a flat surface. Hold her first by her arms, then by her hands, then by her fingers, then let go! Make sure you're close by to catch her when she collapses. Watch her excitement!

Baby's Cognitive Development

Cognitive Manipulation: Although we think of a baby's fingers as fine motor tools, they're also cognitive tools that help a baby learn about her world. She begins to manipulate objects in ways other than grasping, including squeezing, turning, banging, throwing, and transferring.

Expectation: As your baby plays more games, her ability to anticipate the actions and outcomes improves. She loves repeating games because she's anticipating more effectively and she's getting better at the actions and responses.

Object Permanence: By now your baby understands object permanence fairly well. (When something is out of sight, it's not necessarily gone for good.) She hunts for toys when you hide them within her field of vision, and she fusses when you take toys away and try to hide them.

 # How You Can Help

Cognitive Manipulation: Make sure your baby has several interesting objects to manipulate, such as a sponge, playdough, a slice of bread, a squeeze toy, a Koosh ball, a Ping-Pong ball, a rubber ball large enough so she can't swallow it, wrinkled paper, and so on. She can study the objects and learn their different properties.

Expectation: The next time you play a favorite game with your baby, begin the game, but then pause to see if she anticipates what's going to happen next. Proceed with play as usual, but add a new step at the end. See if she learns to anticipate this new step. For example, if you're playing Peek-a-Boo, make a funny face when she pulls the cloth off.

Object Permanence: Play a game with your baby to solidify her awareness of object permanence. Choose two favorite toys and place them in front of her. Cover one toy with a cloth and ask, "Where did it go?" See if she removes the cloth to find it. Repeat with the other toy. Then cover both toys and see what she does. Take the game a step further by hiding the toy behind your back to see if she tries to get it.

Baby's Psychological Development

Fears: If your baby hasn't shown any fears regarding strangers yet, she may still develop them. This simply means she's able to distinguish between familiar people and unfamiliar people. Some babies seem extremely fearful, while others are mildly affected. Don't worry. Your baby will outgrow this.

Exploration: As your baby begins crawling to explore her environment, she may get into things that are dangerous or valuable. She needs as few boundaries as possible (including parents always saying, "No!"), so remove dangerous items ahead of time, but leave plenty of safe things for her to discover. Try to save "No!" for when you really need it.

Caregivers: Babies need to learn to cope with caregivers other than their parents. An occasional babysitter offers your baby a chance to play with someone else, develop independence, and learn new games. Parents get a chance to take a short break, have a night out, and renew their relationship.

 # How You Can Help

Fears: If your baby seems especially fearful of others, she's probably more sensitive. You can help reassure her by keeping her close. She feels more secure knowing you're there. Help her warm up to a stranger by having her share a toy with the person, then let the interaction develop gradually from there.

Exploration: If you don't want "No!" to be your baby's first word, then use it sparingly. Better techniques for helping her stay within safe boundaries include *redirection* (distracting her with something else), *simple explanation* (such as, "That's dangerous. Come over here."), *removing the object or your baby* (so the temptation disappears), and *ignoring the situation* (if the object isn't dangerous and she just wants attention). Guide your baby toward positive behavior by teaching her instead of punishing her.

Caregivers: When leaving your baby with another caregiver, make sure it's someone familiar to her. Have the sitter over to play for a while, and ask the sitter to bring toys to provide your baby with new experiences.

Week 30: Cautiousness

 Baby's Physical Development

Pulling to Standing: As your baby's leg and arm muscles grow stronger, he's able to pull himself to standing using your hands for support and leverage. Soon he'll be pulling himself up using a table, chair, or other object.

Stepping Movements: At the same time your baby begins to stand, he may also begin to make stepping movements by lifting one leg, then the other. What used to be a reflex is now becoming a deliberate attempt to walk.

Weight and Height: Your baby's weight gain and height increase will now slow to about half the rate seen during the first six months. Instead of gaining a pound and a half each month, he'll gain about three-quarters of a pound. Instead of growing an inch each month, he'll grow about half an inch.

 How You Can Help

Pulling to Standing: Help your baby practice pulling himself to standing by offering him your fingers or thumbs to hold onto. You'll feel him tense or straighten his legs as he grasps your fingers. Slowly pull him up, but be ready to catch him if he wobbles. Repeat the action a few times, and soon he'll do it each time he grasps your hands.

Stepping Movements: To help your baby exercise his legs and practice stepping, hold him around his waist while he's standing on the floor. Watch for him to lift a leg. When he does, move him forward a step, then wait for the other leg to lift. In a few weeks you'll be able to hold him by the arms or hands as he steps forward.

Weight and Height: Your baby's regular checkups will provide the information you need to confirm that he's growing at a rate appropriate for him. It doesn't matter if he's larger or smaller than most babies his age, as long as he's growing at a fairly consistent rate. If you have any concerns, talk to your pediatrician.

Baby's Cognitive Development

Hands Together: Your baby may begin to imitate your Pat-a-Cake movement by bringing his hands together at the midpoint. He may also hold a toy in each hand and bang his hands together. This further enhances his understanding of cause and effect. When he bangs things together, he makes a noise.

Responding: Your baby continues to absorb language and may demonstrate understanding of basic words or phrases he hears frequently. He may wave when he hears "bye-bye," look at the door when he hears "Daddy's home," lift his arms when he hears "Want up?" and rub his eyes when he hears "naptime."

Eye-Hand Coordination: As your baby's binocular vision improves along with his ability to imitate movements, he begins to copy some of your simple actions such as clapping, banging the table, and picking up a toy.

 # How You Can Help

Hands Together: Help your baby practice bringing his hands together by clapping his hands while playing Pat-a-Cake. Repeat several times, then give him a chance to clap by himself. He'll soon pick it up. Give him toys he can bang together to make noise. He'll be more apt to repeat an action if there's auditory feedback.

Responding: Help your baby understand simple statements by using gestures to emphasize what you're saying. When it's naptime, make a sleeping gesture. When it's mealtime, make a feeding gesture. Sign language helps increase your baby's receptive and expressive language.

Eye-Hand Coordination: Seat your baby across from you and place a clear plastic bowl within his reach. Place several small toys near the bowl. Pick up one of the toys and drop it in the bowl while saying, "Drop it in!" Gesture for him to do the same. With practice, his imitation skills and eye-hand coordination will improve.

Baby's Psychological Development

Caution: As your baby learns how to use his body to sit, stand, and crawl, he may develop anxieties about his newfound freedom. This internal conflict between freedom and safety will continue for several months. He'll sometimes pull away to explore, and he'll sometimes cling to you for security.

Interpersonal Response: Your baby continues to learn new words and phrases, and he'll soon use this knowledge to express his feelings and relate to others. He still needs lots of input in this area, so be sure to talk to him about what you're doing, how you're feeling, what he's doing, and how he's feeling. This type of communication is called *expressive* language, whereas naming objects is called *referential* language.

Funny Faces: Your baby can imitate your facial expressions not only as a social reference but also for fun. Making faces in person or in the mirror is a great way to express feelings, interact, and have a good time together.

 # How You Can Help

Caution: Allow your baby to decide when he's ready to explore and when he needs reassurance. If you push him into situations he's not ready for, he may become even more anxious and cautious. Your efforts to make him more independent will backfire. Allow him to move at his own pace, give him encouragement along the way, and always support his decision.

Interpersonal Response: In addition to using simple and concrete language that refers to objects, use words and phrases that teach your baby to express his feelings and actions. For example, if he's happy, say, "You're so happy!" If he's hugging you, say, "I love you!" If he's going somewhere, say, "(Baby's name) is going bye-bye."

Funny Faces: Seat your baby opposite you or sit together facing a mirror. Make a series of funny faces and give your baby a chance to imitate each one. Stick out your tongue, puff up your cheeks, wiggle your eyebrows, stretch your mouth open, purse your lips, and so on.

Week 31: Listening

 ## Baby's Physical Development

Nutrition: As your baby continues to grow physically, she probably enjoys more solid foods such as fruits and vegetables. She still gets her primary nutrition from breast milk or formula, but she's beginning to experience new tastes and textures that will soon replace milk as her primary source of nourishment. When you introduce solids, mash the foods so she can manage them. Avoid cow's milk until after the first year, since it doesn't provide the vitamins and iron she needs.

Sitting Alone: Your baby's head and back control are improving, enabling her to sit alone for longer periods with and without support. She may use her hands for support in front of her. If she's not sitting alone yet, continue to give her back support until she's ready to balance on her own.

Self-Feeding: As your baby's fine motor control increases, she's getting better at feeding herself small bits of food. This results from her growing interest in food, her improving eye-hand coordination, and her sense of independence.

 ## How You Can Help

Nutrition: Make feeding time fun by playing games at the highchair, such as Here-Comes-the-Airplane. Hold up a spoon of food, and wave it toward your baby's mouth. Play Open Wide by opening your mouth so she'll imitate you. Play Num-Num by smacking your lips. This isn't the time for teaching manners!

Sitting Alone: To help your baby practice sitting alone, place her in a sitting position without props and support her by sitting opposite her and holding her hands. Play Row-the-Boat by gently pulling her hands back and forth as if she's rowing a boat. She gets a sense of balance, develops better head control, and gains strength in her back.

Self-Feeding: Provide your baby with easy-to-eat foods such as peas, banana slices, cut-up fruit, cut-up soft-cooked vegetables, crackers, and cheese. Don't worry if the food is more a toy than a meal. Eating should be enjoyable, and playing with food should be fun now. Let her play with a spoon so she can practice eating with a utensil.

Baby's Cognitive Development

Goal-Directed Behavior: As your baby continues to learn about cause and effect, she asserts more control over what she wants. She reaches for certain toys, goes after specific objects in the room, gestures for what she needs, and vocalizes for attention. She's learning to master her environment.

Listening: Your baby is listening to specific sounds and sorting them out from others she doesn't recognize. She may practice making sounds by repeating syllables, making up new noises, or "talking" when you talk. She understands more language now, and she distinguishes it from other sounds.

Picture Books: When you read a picture book to your baby, you may notice that she's more attentive to the pictures than the words. She may anticipate the next picture (or even the next sentence) if the book is read to her several times. She may show excitement by vocalizing, slapping the book, or kicking her legs.

 # How You Can Help

Goal-Directed Behavior: Respond to your baby when she gestures or "asks" for something. Give her the words to describe the desired objects or actions and try to provide her with many opportunities to do things for herself. Keep toys within her reach and allow her to crawl around the room freely.

Listening: Play listening games with your baby to enhance her auditory skills. Entertain her with finger plays, songs, and rhymes. Chat with her about what you're doing throughout the day. Continue to use referential language (naming objects as you encounter them) and expressive language (using words for feelings and actions). Her receptive vocabulary is growing rapidly, and in a few short months she'll be saying her first word.

Picture Books: While reading a picture book to your baby, use the opportunity to name the objects in the book. You'll enhance her receptive vocabulary as she listens to you name the objects and watches you point to them. If certain objects make sounds, imitate the sound as you point to the object.

Baby's Psychological Development

Dolls: All babies—boys and girls—need dolls to love, nurture, hold, interact with, and enjoy. Your baby will learn important social, cognitive, and motor skills while playing with dolls. Puppet dolls are especially great at this age, because the parent can interact with the baby through the puppet.

Active Play: Your baby will enjoy more gross motor play now that she's beginning to crawl and stand. Swinging her, flying her over your head, gently bouncing her, and chasing her around will probably cause her to laugh out loud. This type of play is important for all areas of development. She may get so excited she has a hard time relaxing, so you may want to avoid active play right before naptime and bedtime.

Expressing Emotions: Your baby can effectively express four basic emotions at this age: contentment, pleasure, excitement, and unhappiness. She expresses her emotions through vocalizing and body language, but she'll soon express them verbally. Continue to use the words that describe her feelings.

 # How You Can Help

Dolls: Many types of dolls provide learning and nurturing opportunities for your baby, including stuffed animal dolls, baby dolls, lifelike dolls, ethnic dolls, boy and girl dolls, puppet dolls, and so on. When using a puppet, you can talk to your baby, sing a song, act out a silly stunt, and entertain her in a way that increases her attention span. Let her play with the puppet when you're finished interacting, so she gets a chance to think about how it works.

Active Play: Dad is usually the one who engages baby in active play, but mom can, too. A fun game to play is Ride-a-Blanket. Put her on a blanket and pull it around the room—fast enough to be exciting, but not so fast that she might fall off or become frightened.

Expressing Emotions: Play the Emotions game. While sitting across from your baby, make a happy face and say, "Happy!" Also make sad, angry, pleasant, and surprised faces, and name them. Play the game in the mirror for a different experience.

Week 32: Expressing

 Baby's Physical Development

Weight Gain: Your baby's weight gain slows down in the second half of the first year. He takes on less fat for insulation and storage of nourishment, and instead increases bone weight, muscle growth, and overall body development.

Crawling: Your baby is probably getting around fairly well now. He's coordinating his movements for crawling more efficiently. Soon he'll be able to get anywhere in the house, and he may start crawling up or down stairs.

Catch: Amazingly, your baby's ability to reach at this age also includes the ability to catch. He can adjust his reach and catch an object by using eye-hand coordination, depth perception, and coordinated fine and gross motor movements.

 How You Can Help

Weight Gain: If you think your baby is overweight, don't put him on a diet without checking with his pediatrician. He'll most likely outgrow his excess baby fat as he gets taller. Make sure he's getting enough exercise and taking in plenty of milk.

Crawling: To help your baby increase his balance and coordinate his crawling movements, place a few small obstacles in his path for him to maneuver around, over, or through. These might include a chair, a pillow, a folded blanket, or a bunch of soft toys. Make sure you block the stairs both at the top and the bottom, so he doesn't climb without your supervision.

Catch: It's time for your baby's first game of Catch! Set him on the floor propped up so he's stable. Find a lightweight ball about the size of a large cantaloupe. Sit a foot or two opposite him, and simulate the motion of tossing the ball to his midline. Don't actually toss the ball yet, just place it in his hands. Repeat this a few times. When you think he's ready, toss the ball slowly, so it lands in his lap if he misses it. Watch him try to catch it. He may even make contact!

Baby's Cognitive Development

Depth Perception: About this age your baby acquires depth perception. He gains this ability through experience combined with natural development. He'll soon pause when he reaches a step or a ledge, and he may even do so at an incline.

Language Retention: Your baby continues to listen attentively. He's sorting through words and recognizing similar sounds. He's retaining words and sounds longer now, and he'll soon use this information to say his first words.

Increased Interest: Your baby will mostly likely find everything around him interesting. If you place several toys in front of him, he may reach for one, play with it for a few seconds, then move to the next and the next. If there are no toys around, he may play with whatever's within his reach, including his fingers.

 How You Can Help

Depth Perception: To enhance your baby's depth perception, create some simple levels for him to crawl up and down. If you have a stair step, show him how to climb up and get back down. He may be able to climb up easily, but getting down is usually more difficult. He may stop and climb back down before getting to the top. Be sure your staircases are blocked in case he tries to climb when you're not looking.

Language Retention: Experts say the more you read a story to your baby, the more he learns the language and retains the words. Your job is simple and fun: Read the same stories to him over and over. If you wait a few days to reread a story after reading it to him several times, he may show signs of recognizing the speech patterns, sounds, and possibly words. He may widen his eyes, watch your face, flap his arms and legs, and even try to turn the page.

Increased Interest: As your baby's interests increase, give him plenty of opportunities to explore new objects. Take a walk outside and show him whatever you find. Take him to the store and show him all the products. Take him on a field trip and show him the interesting things in his expanding world.

Baby's Psychological Development

Separation Anxiety: About this time your baby may express a fear of being separated from you. This may seem to come out of nowhere, but it's a definite developmental stage. Separation anxiety can be intense for some babies and mild for others. It usually peaks around fourteen to sixteen months, but for some it can last much longer.

Relating to Others: Your baby doesn't realize yet that a person is not a toy. He may grab your hair and pull it, bite your nipple or finger, or reach for another baby's head or hand. He'll be surprised when you say, "No!" or pull back in pain.

Language for Emphasis: Your baby is still learning the words that express emotions, so he continues to use vocalizations, body language, and facial expressions to show his feelings about experiences, toys, and people. You may hear a squeal when he's delighted, a hum when he's content, a giggle when he's excited, a growl or screech when he's angry, and a fuss when he can't express himself any other way.

 # How You Can Help

Separation Anxiety: You can help your baby cope with separation anxiety by introducing new people slowly, by letting him become familiar with new babysitters while you're still there, by leaving with reassurances that you'll come back, by giving him a lovey to keep him secure while you're gone, and by avoiding the "sneak out" method so he isn't confused about your disappearance.

Relating to Others: Your baby will soon begin to understand the difference between objects and people, and he'll realize that parents, siblings, and friends are people just like him. Encourage his emotional response to others by showing him how to pat a crying baby or by smiling when you see his sibling or friend.

Language for Emphasis: Continue using words that describe your baby's feelings, so he can eventually express his emotions with language. Show him human faces that express different emotions, and use the words that describe those feelings. A book of baby faces can be very effective.

Week 33: Separating

 Baby's Physical Development

Thumb-and-Finger Grasp: Watch your baby's hands carefully, and you may notice that she's getting better at grasping objects with her thumb and finger. This skill helps improve her eye-hand coordination and fine motor ability.

Toileting: Your baby may demonstrate awareness of her bladder and bowel by pulling at her diaper or fussing when she has a full diaper. But she's not ready—physically, cognitively, or psychologically—to be toilet trained, and she won't be until she's at least two to two and a half years old.

Lowering to Sit: While your baby is standing and holding your thumbs or a piece of furniture, she may try to lower herself to a sitting position. This is usually deliberate and not necessarily a fall, although it may look a little unco-ordinated.

 How You Can Help

Thumb-and-Finger Grasp: Play Where-Is-Thumbkin? with your baby. Sing the song, and hold up your baby's fingers one-by-one to match each verse, so she becomes aware of each finger and its name. Give her small objects to grasp, such as bits of food, so she practices using her thumb and fingers together.

Toileting: Make diaper changing fun by singing, chanting, or playing. Give her some time to be naked, too. She'll enjoy the chance to crawl around without an interfering diaper, and she'll love the sense of freedom. Diaper time is also a great opportunity to give her a massage.

Lowering to Sit: While your baby is standing, she may bend her legs in an effort to sit. Help lower her to a sitting position by moving your hands down so she doesn't fall too far to the floor. Her padded diaper should cushion her bottom, and with practice and greater leg strength, she'll soon drop to the floor in a smooth and efficient motion.

Baby's Cognitive Development

Visual and Tactile Exploration: Your baby will begin moving from the oral stage of development to the sensory motor stage by increasing her visual and tactile modes of exploring her environment. Instead of using primarily her mouth, she'll use her eyes to see the details of an object and her hands and fingers to feel them. This sensory motor behavior will increase over the next few months.

Tools: Your baby will soon be able to use one object to help her reach or play with another. Her ability to use cause and effect, to solve problems, and to manipulate a tool to achieve a goal are major milestones that lead to more complicated cognitive skills.

Word-Sounds: Although it's still early, your baby may try to shape her vocalizations into nearly recognizable words such as "dah" for daddy or "uh" for up. She may use these word-sounds appropriately one moment and randomly the next. She's thinking generically rather than specifically, and she'll probably use one word for many purposes. On average, babies utter their first word at twelve months.

 # How You Can Help

Visual and Tactile Exploration: Allow your baby to explore new objects. She still uses her mouth quite a bit, so watch her carefully so she doesn't try to swallow something and choke. Let her manipulate the objects, and notice how she coordinates her eyes and hands more. Offer her large-piece puzzles and simple manipulative toys like stacking, nesting, and sorting toys. They're especially good for developing her new modes of exploration.

Tools: Give your baby opportunities to use one object to manipulate another, by setting up simple tasks. Tie a ribbon to a toy, place the toy beyond her reach, and allow her to reach the ribbon. See if she uses it to get the toy. Bury a toy in the sand and give her a toy rake or scoop to uncover it. Do the same thing in the bathtub with a scoop or bowl. Demonstrate a few times, if necessary.

Word-Sounds: To encourage your baby to include word-sounds in her vocalizations, repeat the word-sound she uses when she's referring to something specific. Don't correct her pronunciation or point out her mistakes. She'll fine-tune these word-sounds into actual words as she hears them repeated over time.

Baby's Psychological Development

Relationships with Others: The more your baby trusts her caregivers, the more she trusts other people and develops healthy interpersonal relationships. This is crucial to her success in most areas of life, so be sure she's around nurturing people who care for her and provide her with a secure foundation.

Imitation: Babies are visually aware at this age, and they love to imitate the actions and sounds of other people, especially children. You may notice your baby copying movements or noises while you're doing things around the house.

Negative Emotions: If your baby shows negative emotions such as fear, frustration, or anger, she's responding to situations that elicit these emotions—a normal and healthy developmental response. She's demonstrating her growing range of feelings.

 # How You Can Help

Relationships with Others: Be very careful about leaving your baby with someone else. You want a responsive caregiver who attends to your baby's needs. Interview your sitters thoroughly, ask them questions about how they would handle different situations, and have them spend time with your baby while you're there so you can get a feel for their nurturing skills.

Imitation: When you play with your baby, act out basic skills such as pouring, stacking, banging, and clapping. Then try more complicated tasks such as squeezing dough, folding paper, ringing a bell, and so on. See if she tries to imitate you.

Negative Emotions: Let your baby express her feelings. Don't ignore them or laugh at them. You can teach her healthy ways to express her emotions by modeling appropriate responses to upsetting situations, by redirecting her attention, and by soothing her when she's truly upset. Think how you would feel in her situation and respond the way you would like to be treated.

Week 34: Busyness

 ## Baby's Physical Development

Touching Toes: Your baby is playing with everything he can reach, even his toes. His interest in his environment does not discriminate between his body and the objects around him. He finds anything that moves fascinating.

Banging: As your baby learns how to manipulate the objects in his world, he becomes more enthusiastic in his play. He loves to bang, pound, slap, and shake his toys, and he may even throw them when excited.

Crawling: Your baby's crawling coordination is improving rapidly. Soon he'll be getting from place to place before you realize he can move so fast. His increased speed is a result of his intense desire to be mobile and his improved ability to alternate leg and arm movements.

 ## How You Can Help

Touching Toes: To make your baby's toes even more interesting and fun to play with, draw funny faces on a pair of his white socks using non-toxic felt-tip pens. Slip the socks on his feet and watch him try to reach and grasp them. Sew bells on his socks for added fun.

Banging: Provide your baby with toys that are fun to bang (such as aluminum foil pie pans), fun to shake (such as shakers and bells), fun to slap (such as plastic bubble wrap), and fun to throw (such as musical balls and stuffed animals).

Crawling: Double-check your baby's play area regularly to make sure it's safe for him to explore freely. Set up goals for him to reach by placing toys throughout the play area. Continue playing games of chase, such as Gonna-Get-You, and providing manageable obstacles for him to overcome.

Baby's Cognitive Development

Word Recognition: Talking to your baby is paying off as he absorbs more and more language. He's now able to recognize several words that he hears on a regular basis. He shows recognition by looking at the object, making an appropriate gesture, or trying to imitate the sound of the word.

Sound Recognition: Your baby is less likely to be startled by sounds that previously caused fear or fussiness, such as a vacuum cleaner, a toilet flushing, a dog barking, or a door slamming. He's learning that the sounds won't hurt him and he's losing the startle (Moro) reflex.

Body Recognition: Your baby is still learning the distinction between his body and his environment. Sometimes he uses his body parts to get what he wants. He uses his hands to grasp things, his legs to kick and move, and his head to locate sounds and sights. At other times he doesn't seem to know where his body parts end and his environment begins. He plays with his body as if it were a toy.

 # How You Can Help

Word Recognition: Play a word recognition game with your baby by selecting three of his favorite toys. Place them a few inches apart and within his reach. Say the name of one toy and watch his reaction. Does he look at it, reach for it, or vocalize? Show him the toy, repeat the word, then give it to him. Repeat with the other toys. Play a few days later to see if his word recognition improves.

Sound Recognition: As your baby recognizes more and more sounds, he's beginning to anticipate the causes of the sounds. He may show excitement by kicking, vocalizing, or trying to move toward an object making a sound. Play the Hidden Sound game by choosing three objects that make different sounds. Place the objects behind a small screen and make a sound with one. Remove the screen and see if he reaches for the correct object.

Body Recognition: To help your baby learn the distinction between his body and his environment, play the Sticker Game. Place a large colorful sticker on his arm, hand, leg, or tummy. Try the sticker on your body first to make sure it doesn't hurt when it comes off. Name the body part attached to the sticker and see how he responds. He may look at it, grasp it, or have some other reaction.

Baby's Psychological Development

Showing Affection: Your baby likes to be with you and will show signs of affection by grasping your hand, hugging you, smiling at you, gesturing to be picked up, and fussing when you leave the room or put him down. He may even imitate giving you a kiss if you kiss him a lot.

Self-Awareness: Your baby is learning more about himself as a separate being. He can now imitate movements involving his body parts when demonstrated by another person, such as touching his head, toes, or tummy.

Emotional Range: Your baby's emotional range is increasing. He's fine-tuning his emotional expressions and learning from others by watching their expressions. He asserts himself by reaching for something he wants, protests if he's unhappy with something by pushing it away, shows fear by crying or turning away, and laughs when he wants an action repeated.

 # How You Can Help

Showing Affection: Play Gimme-a-Kiss to teach your baby one way of expressing his affection. Hold him in your lap facing you and say, "Who wants a kiss?" Then say, "Baby wants a kiss!" Lean in and give him a kiss. Repeat several times. See if he starts to lean in or makes a kissing gesture.

Self-Awareness: A good way to enhance your baby's self-awareness is a game called Where's Baby? Place your baby on the floor and cover him with a small blanket or towel. See if he tries to pull off the cover to reveal himself. Place him in a large cardboard box, cover the top with a towel, and see if he tries to let you know he's inside.

Emotional Range: Your baby is still demonstrating his feelings with gestures and vocalizations, but continue to give him simple words to help him identify his feelings and communicate them through language. Make faces in the mirror and give the faces names that describe their emotional significance.

Week 35: Experimenting

 Baby's Physical Development

Sitting Up: As your baby's back muscles get stronger and her desire to keep moving increases, she may be able to get up to a sitting position from lying on her back. She'll most likely accomplish this by rolling over to one side and lifting herself up or by rolling to her tummy and pushing herself up.

Teeth: Some babies have a few teeth by this time, while others are still toothless. The top two teeth or bottom two teeth should appear any time now, in either order. There's a wide range of normal in this area, so don't be concerned about your baby's teeth at this point.

Sitting Steady: Your baby's balance will improve if she's given time to practice sitting alone. Set her on a soft blanket or carpet, surround her with toys to keep her occupied, and she may sit for some time without falling over.

 How You Can Help

Sitting Up: If your baby hasn't figured out how to move to a sitting position from lying on her back, practice a few techniques with her. Place her on her back, roll her to her side, and lift her gently by the top arm to a sitting position. Repeat the exercise, this time rolling her to her tummy and encouraging her to push herself up to sitting. This is a good exercise and a fun skill to learn.

Teeth: Although your baby has probably been drooling for weeks, she's been relatively pain free. But as her teeth begin to break through, she may start to fuss more. Provide her with firm, cold toys or teethers to chew on, and rub her gums with numbing medication to ease the pain. As soon as the tooth breaks through, she'll feel better. If she bites during a feeding, pull back and say, "Ouch!" to remind her not to bite.

Sitting Steady: If your baby still needs to be propped up, make sure she feels secure, to help her confidence and balance. Slowly remove the prop and place a few fingers at her back for balance. Keep her occupied with toys, so her focus is on what she's doing instead of how she's sitting. Slowly release your fingers and let her find her center. Stay close in case she starts to fall.

Baby's Cognitive Development

Attention Span: Until now your baby's attention span has been brief. She has rapidly transferred her focus from toy to toy, from person to person, and from emotion to emotion. But now she may begin to focus longer on a toy or activity. She may find a lively TV show fascinating to watch for several minutes. Make sure the content is appropriate.

Experimenting: Your baby should be able to use simple cause-and-effect exploration to experiment with objects. She may try to take something apart, make it perform in a different way, or combine it with another toy to see what happens.

Problem Solving: Your baby is watching you and learning from what she sees. Her ability to imitate your actions enables her to solve problems, try new techniques, move in new ways, and learn new skills. Show her how you solve simple problems throughout the day.

 # How You Can Help

Attention Span: To help your baby improve her attention span, find a quiet place with few distractions. Sit close to her and sing a song, enjoy a finger play, or perform with a puppet. Extend the play by creating new verses, adding new toys, imagining new scenarios, and so on. You'll find her attention lasts longer each day.

Experimenting: Offer your baby objects that are fun to explore, and she'll begin to experiment with them. Watch her investigate the properties of a peeled banana. Playdough is fun to explore, but make sure she doesn't put it in her mouth. Offer her any kind of toy that comes apart or changes into something else, as long as it's safe.

Problem Solving: Allow your baby the opportunity to watch you perform tasks, and encourage her to imitate you. For example, when you brush your teeth, let her watch you while she holds a small toothbrush. If you're folding laundry, let her sit with you near the laundry pile and copy your movements with a washcloth or sock.

Baby's Psychological Development

Experiencing Feelings: As your baby watches you throughout the day, she recognizes your facial expressions and moods and she tries to imitate them. The more intense your feelings, the more sensitive your baby will be to them. If you smile and laugh a lot, your baby is more likely to do the same. If you're upset and angry, your baby will copy these emotions.

Emotional Vocalizations: Listen to the differences in your baby's tone and pitch when she vocalizes. If she's upset, her syllables and sounds will be harsh, low, and angry. If she's happy, they're more likely to be high-pitched and joyful.

Fear of Being Alone: Around this time your baby may suddenly be afraid to be alone for a few minutes or to go to bed by herself. This is a common developmental stage. Realizing she's alone means your baby is developing a sense of self. She knows she's separate from her loved ones, and this can be scary for her.

 # How You Can Help

Experiencing Feelings: It's not easy being happy all day, but if you remember how much your baby senses your feelings, you'll make an extra effort to smile and laugh and check yourself when you're angry or sad. If you find you're getting tense, take a break or play with your baby. That should cheer you up!

Emotional Vocalizations: Tell your baby a story by using puppets. Have one puppet speak in a high voice and the other speak in a low voice. Watch your baby's facial expressions as she listens to the different voices. Listen to her vocalizations throughout the day for appropriate pitch and tone.

Fear of Being Alone: If your baby becomes frightened when you need to leave the room, talk to her from other parts of the house to reassure her you're coming back. If she's fearful at bedtime, leave a night-light on, put a few toys in her bed, and let her play herself to sleep. You can also reassure her by singing her a song and patting her for a few minutes. If she becomes hysterical when you're gone, return to her room and comfort her.

Week 36: Standing

 Baby's Physical Development

Standing Alone: At around nine months some babies can stand alone momentarily. As your baby spreads his legs apart for stability, he probably appears bow-legged and precarious, but in fact he's finding his balance point. This is the next step toward walking, which occurs on average at twelve months.

Walking Assisted: Your baby may begin to take steps while standing and holding your hands. His gait will be awkward and marching-like, and he may try to move faster than he's able, which will cause him to lose his balance.

Pincer Grasp: Your baby should be getting better at retrieving small objects from the carpet, floor, and lawn with his thumb and forefinger. Watch him to make sure he doesn't put choking hazards in his mouth.

 How You Can Help

Standing Alone: Help your baby practice standing alone by placing him on a flat surface and holding his hands so he can find his balance. Reassure him until you feel he's ready to stand on his own, then slowly let go of his hands. Giving him a toy to hold may help by distracting him from what he's doing.

Walking Assisted: Begin by holding both of your baby's hands and guiding him across the floor. Follow his lead. As he gets better, try holding only one hand and see if he can continue walking. Give him something to hold in the other hand. This may give him the balance and distraction he needs.

Pincer Grasp: To improve your baby's pincer grasp, let him practice picking up small objects. Small bits of food are best, because he can put them in his mouth. He can also practice with non-edible items, as long as you watch him closely. He'll eventually try to put them in his mouth.

Baby's Cognitive Development

Deferred Imitation: Your baby's memory is improving, and he may now be able to remember and imitate behaviors he's seen but not experienced personally. For example, if he sees another child playing with a toy one day, he may be able to play with it the same way the next day. This is a big step in his cognitive development.

Deduction Skills: As your baby's understanding of cause and effect improves, he begins to demonstrate simple deduction skills. For example, he may figure out how to get a toy that's not within his reach, if there's a simple solution such as using a blanket to pull it toward him or removing an obstacle to obtain it.

Object Permanence: Your baby takes object permanence to a new level around this age. He searches for an object he sees you hide, which means he understands the object has not disappeared and he can find it.

 # How You Can Help

Deferred Imitation: Give your baby the chance to improve his memory by showing him a new toy. Demonstrate how to play with it, then put it away. Bring it out several hours later, and see if he remembers how to play with it. If he doesn't, show him again. After he's finished playing with it, put it away until the next day. Then bring it out and see if he remembers how to play with it.

Deduction Skills: Help your baby solve problems by setting up challenging activities. Place him in his highchair next to a table. Spread a blanket on the table within his reach. Place a toy at the far end of the blanket. See if he can figure out how to get the toy. You can also place an obstacle, such as a book, in his way, so he has to remove it or maneuver around it.

Object Permanence: Play Hide-and-Seek with your baby. Place him on the floor, then take one of his toys and hide it a short distance away in an accessible place. Make sure he sees you hide the toy, so he can find it. Ask him, "Where's the (toy)?" See if he tries to find it. Repeat with different toys in different places.

Baby's Psychological Development

Pleasing: Your baby has become aware of your feelings to the extent that he may try to please you by performing a task and looking to you for a smile or praise. This shows he's developing a sense of self and an understanding of basic emotions.

Body Awareness: As your baby develops more body awareness, he begins to use parts of his body to get what he wants or communicate his needs and desires. For example, if you try to wash his face, he may cover it with his hands if he doesn't feel like getting washed. If he's about to be changed and isn't in the mood, he may wiggle and squirm to prevent it.

Name Recognition: Your baby's name is important to him, and he should be responding to it by now, if you're using it frequently. He's also able to respond to simple commands connected to his name, such as "No, (baby's name)!" and "Bye-bye, (baby's name)."

 # How You Can Help

Pleasing: Since your baby is already trying to please you, make sure you praise him through language and facial expressions. Ask him to perform a simple task such as picking up a toy or waving bye-bye. After he completes the task, say, "Good job!" and smile as you make eye contact. If you don't give your child positive feedback, it could inhibit his desire to improve his skills.

Body Awareness: Play body-awareness games to encourage your baby's ability to recognize and manipulate his gross and fine motor skills. Place a sticker on his hand and see if he tries to take it off. Place it on another part of his body and see if he searches for it. Tuck a small toy under his clothes and see if he tries to retrieve it.

Name Recognition: Use your baby's name as often as you can, so he learns it well. While looking in the mirror together, point to him and say his name. Then point to yourself and say, "mommy" or "daddy." Use the names of family members so he can learn those, too.

Week 37: Playfulness

 Baby's Physical Development

Holding Objects: At this age your baby might be able to hold three small toys at once. This skill takes more coordination and thought, so it may be a challenge at first. She'll probably need a few tries to figure out how to manage that extra toy with only two hands.

Turning Pages: A more difficult skill your baby may try is turning the pages of a book. This requires the ability to use her fingers to pick up something flat (not an easy task). Using her hand and wrist to turn a page without tearing it presents another challenge.

Standing Holding On: Around the time your baby learns to stand while holding your hands, she takes another developmental step by pulling herself to standing while holding furniture. This may make her feel insecure initially, but her desire to stand motivates her to take chances.

 How You Can Help

Holding Objects: Give your baby a small toy to hold. After a few seconds give her a second toy and watch her hold one in each hand. After a few seconds hand her a third toy and see what she does. She may drop one toy, try to hold two toys in one hand, or ignore the third toy. If she doesn't manage to hold all the toys, try again a few days later to see if she responds differently.

Turning Pages: Give your baby a cloth book first and let her experiment with turning pages. Then give her a cardboard book and see how she manages. Then give her an inexpensive picture book and see how she does.

Standing Holding On: Encourage your baby to stand without your help by placing her near a couch, sturdy chair, or coffee table. Slowly transfer her hands from your hands to the furniture. Remain close by to catch her if she loses her balance. Cover all sharp table corners with protective guards to keep her from hurting herself if she falls against them.

Baby's Cognitive Development

Visual Comparison: As your baby holds objects in both of her hands, she continues to assess and compare them. She holds the items close together, looks back and forth between them, and mouths them to learn even more.

Auditory Discrimination: Your baby listens to the sounds in her environment and discriminates between those that are important to her and those that are not. She recognizes many different voices and meaningful household sounds, and she's able to learn the differences among new sounds she's not familiar with, such as animal sounds.

Intentional Behavior: The major development in your baby's cognitive skills at this stage is doing things on purpose instead of randomly. Her behaviors and actions *mean* something now. She's making an effort to perform tasks that she enjoys. This intentional behavior enables her to learn more about cause and effect and problem solving, and each discovery builds on what she's previously learned.

 # How You Can Help

Visual Comparison: Help your baby learn to compare things by offering her two dissimilar items to study, such as a small ball and a block. Then offer similar items, such as two balls of different sizes, colors, or textures. Watch her reaction to see if she notices the differences or shows a preference. Give her lots of similar and different items to compare.

Auditory Discrimination: Expand your baby's auditory discrimination skills by introducing her to new sounds. Find a book that features common animals such as a chicken, cow, lion, and pig. Imitate the animal sounds as you show her the pictures. Repeat this activity over several days and see if she begins to recognize or repeat the sounds.

Intentional Behavior: Watch your baby for a few minutes to see what she does. Try to figure out why she's doing certain tasks or playing certain games. What's the motivation behind her behavior? It's fun to interpret the thought processes that inspire your baby's actions.

Baby's Psychological Development

Attention Span: As the world becomes more interesting and accessible to your baby, her attention span increases. She may be able to focus on a toy or task for several minutes now, if it provides enough stimulation to keep her occupied.

Purposeful Communication: Your baby will probably begin to direct meaningful vocalizations at specific people now, even though they may not be able to understand her intentions. She's trying to have a conversation, not just get their attention, and she may become frustrated if they don't respond.

Social Interaction: Your baby may use social interaction to solve a problem she can't solve on her own. For example, she may lift up a container she wants to open but can't, indicating her need for your help.

 # How You Can Help

Attention Span: Try to keep your baby's playthings interesting and stimulating. If she starts to lose interest in a toy, show her another way to play with it. For example, she may enjoy rolling a ball, but you might show her how to bounce it, catch it, or throw it. See if she plays with it longer in these new ways. Some parents rotate toys by putting some away for a while. When the toys are brought out again, the baby thinks they're brand-new.

Purposeful Communication: When your baby seems to be initiating a conversation with you, respond to her by using her speech sounds or by saying the words she's trying to say. For example, you might be able to tell if she's asking a question by her tone of voice or facial expression. Repeat the sound, point to the object she's trying to indicate, and add a word or two such as, "Want the ball?" or "Throw the ball?"

Social Interaction: Watch your baby for cues (vocalizations or gestures) that she's trying to communicate with you, especially when she's trying to solve a problem. Before you provide the solution, give her a chance to solve the problem on her own by making the solution easier to achieve. For example, break the task into steps, such as loosening the top to a container she wants opened, then let her finish the task.

Week 38: Feeding

 ## Baby's Physical Development

Feeding: As your baby becomes used to new foods, he's more apt to try to feed himself with his fingers or a spoon, although probably not with great coordination. He's capable of eating mashed or strained food directly from the dinner table, but it's best not to add salt or other additives.

Grasp Release: Until now your baby hasn't had the ability to deliberately let go of an object in his hand. His reflexive grasp has been automatic, and he's had difficulty relaxing that grasp. But now he should be able to let go of a toy by dropping it, throwing it, or setting it down.

Supported Steps: When you give your baby the opportunity to stand supported by you or nearby furniture, you may see him attempt to take a step by lifting one leg and putting it down again. He may not walk unassisted for another several weeks, but he's already practicing.

 ## How You Can Help

Feeding: Feeding time should be pleasurable for your baby. Let him enjoy his food by using all his senses. He may want to squish it, spread it, pound it, smell it, even taste it! Feeding time can be an excellent learning opportunity.

Grasp Release: Help your baby practice releasing his grip by offering him a toy, then offering another and another to encourage him to release his grip. If he has trouble, gently unpeel his fingers to enhance his awareness of his fine motor ability. Play Open-Them-Shut-Them, a game in which you open and close your hands while encouraging your baby to do the same.

Supported Steps: Have your baby stand in a well-balanced position with his legs comfortably apart. Let him hold your fingers and find his center point. Gently move one arm forward, causing his shoulder and eventually his leg to follow. Then move the other arm. Repeat until he gets tired of the exercise.

Baby's Cognitive Development

Jabbering: You may notice a difference in your baby's vocalizations as he gets closer to saying his first real word. He may start to jabber by using vocal inflections and tones that sound like real speech and are accompanied by gestures. Jabbering further indicates your baby's strong desire to express himself specifically and effectively.

In and Out: Your baby's interactions with his environment help increase his cognitive skills, and he's beginning to understand the concepts of in and out. In order to do this, he must understand other basic concepts such as object permanence, cause and effect, problem solving, and initiative.

Cognitive Exploration: Your baby will use new and learned techniques to explore objects within his reach. He may bang or hit them, shake or throw them, squeeze or smash them, or even try to pull them apart—all in an effort to learn more about them.

 # How You Can Help

Jabbering: Pay careful attention to your baby's jabbering and attempt to interpret what he's trying to say. Respond to him by repeating what he says, by pointing to the object(s) he's referring to, and by acting out your interpretation of his comment or your answer to his question. Gradually his expressions will become clearer.

In and Out: To help your baby understand these new concepts, give him a small box with a lid. Let him see you place a toy in the box, then close the box. Place the box within his reach and see what he does. If he needs help figuring out what to do, open the box and show him the toy inside. Repeat several times, then try again in a few days.

Cognitive Exploration: Give your baby objects that encourage his investigation, so he can apply his learned skills and discover new ones. For example, give him a wooden spoon to bang on a pan, a container of sprinkles to shake, a piece of bread to squish, a toy hammer to pound, a puzzle to take apart, and so on.

Baby's Psychological Development

Attachment: At this time some babies grow increasingly attached to a toy, stuffed animal, blanket, or pacifier. These objects offer security when your baby needs it. A lovey provides comfort when a parent is gone, when a babysitter arrives, or when a new situation arises.

Affection: Your baby is becoming increasingly mobile and independent, and he may not seem to require as much affection from you as he did weeks ago. However, he still needs lots of love and attention, even if he doesn't show it.

Mirror Time: Your baby is making great strides in self-awareness. You should continue mirror play so he can further distinguish between himself and you. He can watch his body move and recognize himself in the reflection.

 # How You Can Help

Attachment: If your baby doesn't seem to have an attachment to a lovey, provide him with opportunities to bond with something he can keep handy when he needs it. Put him to bed with a favorite stuffed animal, give him the same blanket to cuddle with, and allow him to have his pacifier as long as he needs it. You're not making him dependent, you're doing just the opposite—encouraging his independence.

Affection: Hug and kiss your baby at least ten times a day. That's the recommended dose of love he needs to keep him happy and confident as he explores his world. Play games, chat, go on field trips, sit together and read, or just hold him in your lap so he knows you're there.

Mirror Time: To increase your baby's self-awareness, add some new activities to Mirror Time. While he's looking in the mirror, put a sticker on his face. Point to his face in the mirror, then point to his actual face, and see if he makes the connection. Put a hat on your head, then take the hat off, and put it on his head. See if he takes it off and tries to put it back on you. Sit behind him with your face hidden, move your arms at his sides, and see if he's intrigued by his "extra" arms.

Week 39: Egocentrism

 Baby's Physical Development

Bottle, Spoon, and Cup: Around this age your baby has the fine motor ability to hold her own bottle and drink from it. She can also grasp a spoon, although keeping food on it may still be tricky. And she can now manage a cup with liquid in it, but there will likely be frequent spills, unless you give her a sippy cup that helps prevent spills.

Stepping Assisted: As your baby practices standing while holding your hand or the furniture, she may try to take a step. She's not quite ready to let go, but she may manage one step unassisted before falling.

Eye-Hand Coordination: Your baby's fine motor skills are increasing rapidly. She's beginning to place objects in specific places with greater coordination. This leads to sorting and greater finger control.

 How You Can Help

Bottle, Spoon, and Cup: Give your baby opportunities to hold her bottle from time to time, but don't give up that special cuddling time completely. Also offer her a baby spoon at mealtime and show her how to use it. Have her practice using a spoon by letting her scoop peas and put them into a cup or bowl. And let her handle her cup without the cap on top. In the bath let her practice pouring water from a cup to another container.

Stepping Assisted: While your baby is standing, you may feel her trying to move forward by twisting her body and lifting her legs. Help her along by holding her hands and letting her practice walking. If you want to let go for a moment, have someone opposite her motivate her to move forward. But be ready to catch her when she falls.

Eye-Hand Coordination: Set half an egg carton in front of your baby and place a small toy in each of the six cups. Remove the toys and set them in front of her. Point to a toy, then to a cup, and see if she places the toy inside the cup. Guide her by saying, "Put the toy in the cup."

Baby's Cognitive Development

Matching: Your baby has the cognitive ability to associate objects based on experience. For example, she knows the rubber nipple belongs on the bottle, the hat goes on the doll, and the shoes go with the socks. This is an important skill that helps her organize her world.

Problem Solving: Your baby continues to be active and interested in her surroundings, but occasionally she confronts obstacles that impede her progress. She uses problem-solving skills she's learned through experience, and ones she discovers on the spot, to overcome these barriers.

Receptive Language: By the time your baby is a year old, she'll probably have a receptive vocabulary of fifty words. That means right now she can understand thirty to forty words and phrases you use frequently. She understands much more language than she's able to express.

 # How You Can Help

Matching: Gather objects that go together, such as the ones mentioned above, or toys that are similar, such as puzzle pieces, balls, blocks, and dolls. Set three different objects in front of your baby and name them. Then set three matching objects next to their pairs. Remove one of each pair and set them to the side. Hold up one object and ask, "Where's the other (object)?" See if she can indicate which one is the match.

Problem Solving: Set up barriers for your baby to overcome, so she can practice solving problems. Don't make the barriers too difficult or frustrating, or she'll give up. For example, set a new toy at the other end of the room. Place some obstacles in her path, such as pillows, a chair, cushions, a table, and so on. Watch how she maneuvers around them. If she needs help, show her a way to solve the problem.

Receptive Language: In addition to introducing new words, try to repeat common words and phrases when interacting with your baby. To see how much she understands, say some frequently used words, and watch for her appropriate responses. She may wave when she hears, "bye-bye," get her blanket when she hears, "bedtime," and look for her dolly when she hears, "Where's baby?"

Baby's Psychological Development

Egocentrism: Your baby will think she's the center of the universe for the next couple of years, as her sense of self develops. She's learning about what she can do, how others feel about her, and how she feels about herself.

Laughter: Your baby probably laughs out loud when engaged in gross motor play such as Airplane, Gonna-Get-You, and Ride-a-Horsy. She loves the occasional surprise from Peek-a-Boo, as long as it's not too startling.

Name Recognition: Your baby should be recognizing her name when you use it. She may lift her head toward the sound of your voice, answer back by trying to repeat her name, or show recognition in her facial expression.

 # How You Can Help

Egocentrism: As your baby's sense of self develops, she's more apt to hold onto a toy if you try to take it away and she's likely to cry when you do. She lets you know what she wants and doesn't want. If she has a special toy and doesn't want anyone to play with it, let her have it exclusively. She's not being selfish. She's establishing her sense of self.

Laughter: Continue playing your baby's favorite games to make her laugh, and add new ones to encourage a new range of happy emotions. Try Where's Baby? Encourage her to hide, then creep around on all fours until you find her. Call out, "There she is!" and enjoy her laugh.

Name Recognition: Use your baby's name a lot, so she becomes quite familiar with it. Call her from across the room, and wave to her when she sees you. When you give her a toy, say, "This is for (baby's name)!" If you have older children, include your baby's name in a family roll call when setting the table, so she knows she's part of the group.

Week 40: Daring

 Baby's Physical Development

Lowering to Sit: Now that your baby's leg muscles are getting stronger, he'll soon be able to lower himself from a standing position to a sitting position without falling. He'll probably use part of the furniture to help him, which shows his problem-solving skills as well.

Foot Development: Your baby's flat feet are showing no signs of arches yet, but over time they will become arched, unless they're genetically programmed to remain flat. He needs plenty of barefoot time when practicing standing, because it's easier to stand and walk with bare feet.

Sitting Steady: Sitting alone should be well established at this age. While in a sitting position, your baby can lean over and pick up a toy, hold a toy in each hand, turn his body to locate a sound, and remain sitting for longer periods while entertaining himself.

 How You Can Help

Lowering to Sit: Help your baby practice getting into a sitting position from standing. While holding his hands, place him in a standing position. Slowly lower your hands and guide him to a sitting position. Motivate him to sit, if necessary, by placing a toy on the floor in front of him. After a few times, position him near the furniture to practice on his own.

Foot Development: Give your baby a foot massage to help him become more aware of his feet and to help his feet relax when he's not kicking, standing, and stepping. Let him go barefoot as much as possible.

Sitting Steady: Increase your baby's sitting time by providing him lots of toys to choose from and play with while he's sitting. Have him sit on a variety of surfaces to challenge his sitting balance. These may include a couch, a table, the lawn, a pillow, and so on. Help him find his balance on each surface, and be sure to stay nearby in case he tips.

Baby's Cognitive Development

Goal-Directed Behavior: Your baby has made many strides in cognitive development. He anticipates repeated events and learns to adapt to new situations. Also, his actions tend to be goal-directed, for the most part. In other words, there's a reason for most of his actions and vocalizations.

Hide and Seek: Your baby's understanding of object permanence is well established. He loves to uncover objects to find something, and he loves to hide and have someone find him. As his cognitive skills continue to develop, he'll soon be able to find objects that require more seeking.

Interest in Detail: As your baby explores objects, he's now noticing details beyond size, shape, and color. You may see him looking at a toy up close, turning it around to see it from all sides, and picking at some part of it to see if it will come off.

 # How You Can Help

Goal-Directed Behavior: Watch your baby's actions to see if you can read what's motivating him. If he gets his blanket, it may mean he wants to take a nap. Give him the words that describe his actions, and help him follow through with the task, if necessary.

Hide and Seek: You can expand Hide-and-Seek in various ways. Hide a small toy under a cup or bowl and let your baby find it. Hide yourself somewhere in the room and let him find you. Hide objects under blankets and pillows, inside boxes, under hats, and so on. He may even want to hide himself under a sheet or blanket or curtain. He'll have lots of fun revealing himself to you. Encourage other caregivers to play as well.

Interest in Detail: Offer your baby toys and objects that are complex and enticing, so he can increase his ability to distinguish various details. Dolls with interesting faces, blocks with designs, picture books with attractive illustrations, and "manipulatives" with lots of parts are best. Be sure the objects don't have detachable parts that could pose a choking hazard.

Baby's Psychological Development

Fear of Strangers: Even if your baby has been outgoing and receptive to most people thus far, he may suddenly show a fear of strangers at this age. Such behavior is based on temperament and varies from baby to baby. Fear of strangers is related to separation anxiety (a baby's fear of being left by his parent and caregiver). Babies outgrow these fears eventually, some more slowly than others.

Breastfeeding: Your baby may lose interest in breastfeeding around this time, if he hasn't already. As more foods are introduced to him, he may become less interested in milk and may begin to wean himself. However, he may still cling to the bedtime feeding for another few weeks or months.

Talking: Your baby continues to fine-tune his vocalizations, and he uses more of the same sounds or "words" to convey his meaning. These vocalizations are usually accompanied by gestures, which help him show his intent.

 # How You Can Help

Fear of Strangers: Help your baby get through this period of emotional development by approaching strangers slowly and cautiously. Be sensitive to your baby's facial expressions and body language as you approach people. If he reacts by clinging or crying, let him stay near you, and reassure him with words like, "It's okay" or "He's nice." If your baby is reluctant to go with a stranger, don't force him, if at all possible. For example, don't let your friend hold him just to please your friend, if your baby doesn't want to be held by your friend.

Breastfeeding: If your baby wants to wean himself, there's not much you can do. Try to do it gradually instead of all at once, so it's easier on your breasts. You can often maintain the bedtime feeding after other times have been eliminated. It's an important cuddling time for both of you. As he weans himself, make sure he's getting enough milk from the bottle or cup, and continue to use formula, not cow's milk, until he's at least a year old.

Talking: Try to listen to your baby as he "talks," and respond to his requests as best you can. If you're not clear on his meaning, it may turn into a guessing game, but eventually you'll connect through trial and error.

Week 41: Silliness

 ## Baby's Physical Development

Back Rolling: It's easier for your baby to roll from her tummy to her back than from her back to her tummy. She may also try to roll up into a sitting position from her back, another big accomplishment.

Grasp Release: Your baby is still practicing her grasp release and gaining more control over her fine motor muscles. She may still throw or drop things at random, but she may also be able to give you a toy by deliberately letting go of it when you take it from her.

One Foot: At this age your baby probably enjoys standing and perhaps taking a step with assistance. She may even be able to stand on one foot for a few seconds.

 ## How You Can Help

Back Rolling: To encourage your baby to roll from her back to her tummy or into a sitting position, give her lots of floor time on her back, free of restrictions. Place a toy on either side of her, so she has an incentive to roll over. Give her a little support at her back while tucking in her arm in front, to help propel her body.

Grasp Release: To help your baby practice her grasp release, give her a toy to play with for a while. When she seems ready to give it up, reach for it, gently grasp it, and see if she lets go. You can also ask her for the toy. If she releases it, make sure to say, "Thank you." Repeat this activity from time to time, but not too often—she'll think you want all her toys!

One Foot: While your baby is practicing standing, encourage her to stand on one foot. Have her stand holding a piece of furniture, then lift one of her feet briefly. See she if can hold her weight for a few seconds. Repeat with the other foot. You can also say, "Lift your foot" to give her the language to go with the action.

Baby's Cognitive Development

Names: Your baby is growing more and more aware of her name, so continue to use it often. She's also learning the names of others, so use those as well. Try to avoid "she," "him," "we," or "them," whenever possible. This will help her identify familiar people and further sort out her world.

Concept Association: Your baby is applying concepts she's already learned to ones she's now learning. For example, if you give her a new rattle that's similar to but different from her familiar rattle, she may shake it immediately just as she would with her familiar rattle. She's applying what she's learned to a new experience.

Vocabulary: Your baby is absorbing more vocabulary, and she'll soon be expressing herself verbally. She's probably learned "mama" and "dada" and some basic concepts such as "bye-bye," "juice," "blanket," "pacifier," "doggy," "night-night," "hi," and of course "no."

 # How You Can Help

Names: Play name games with your baby to increase her awareness of people's identities. When a new friend appears, use the person's name frequently so she can learn it. When several people are in the room, point to a person when you use his or her name. Occasionally ask your baby, "Where's (name)?" and see if she can identify the person by pointing to him or her, by going over to the person, or by looking at him or her.

Concept Association: Give your baby new toys that are similar to familiar ones and see what she does with them. For example, give her a new doll and see if she handles it as she handles her old doll. Give her a toy truck and see if she plays with it as she plays with her toy car. Before showing her different ways to play with a new toy, let her interact with it to see what she discovers on her own.

Vocabulary: Continue expanding your baby's vocabulary by using simple words and sentences that describe her everyday experiences. Whenever possible, accompany the words with gestures to make the ideas more concrete. Soon you'll hear your baby speak her first word! Which one will it be?

Baby's Psychological Development

Independence: When you say, "No!" to your baby, she may initially respond by pulling back, by stopping what she's doing, or by crying if she's startled. She may continue doing what she's doing, even though she knows she's not supposed to. She's showing her independence and testing her boundaries. She may even look at you when she's doing something she knows she shouldn't, which reveals her awareness of your rules and boundaries.

Changing Time: Changing your baby may become more challenging now, as she struggles to be free while you struggle with her diaper and clothing. She's increasingly mobile and more curious than ever, and she wants to get on with playing. She may be less cooperative at feeding time, too.

Silly Time: Your baby enjoys laughing when you're being silly, and she begins to show signs of being silly herself. Respond to her odd noises, funny faces, and silly antics by laughing with her. Laughter has a definite impact on her mood and personality, so keep the good times rolling.

 # How You Can Help

Independence: Your baby will be asserting herself now and won't always respond favorably to what she's asked or told. Try to appreciate her independence and the fact that she's thinking for herself instead of blindly obeying a rule. Baby-proof your home to prevent unnecessary confrontations over dangerous objects, provide positive alternatives when she's doing something you don't want her to do, and try to use "No!" sparingly. Follow through when you tell her not to do something, and give her the opportunity to shake her head "No!" from time to time.

Changing Time: Make changing time fun by playing games, singing songs, reciting rhymes, turning on the mobile, and giving your baby interesting objects to examine. As long as she's occupied, she's more likely to cooperate.

Silly Time: Encourage your baby's sense of humor by giving her funny hats to put on while she's looking at herself in the mirror. Play silly games and do lots of giggling while you play. Make faces, use funny voices, pretend to fall or spill things—whatever makes her laugh and encourages her sense of humor.

Week 42: Learning

 ## Baby's Physical Development

Balance: Your baby is developing many new skills that require balance. He's probably tipping over and falling down quite a bit, but he's making every effort to establish his balance. He throws his arms out, tries to center his head, flexes his knees, and does his best to maintain an upright position.

Stepping: Your baby especially likes standing and walking with your assistance. It's a fairly new skill that's very exciting to perform! He's eager to take an unassisted step, but that won't happen for another few weeks for most babies. The average age for walking unassisted is twelve months. Some babies walk at nine months, while others wait until eighteen months or longer.

Roughhousing: There are many reasons why your baby loves roughhousing. He gets to exercise his gross motor muscles; he has fun chasing, swinging, and tumbling with you; and he laughs a lot! Roughhousing is a particularly fun way to interact with your baby, but use caution. He's still somewhat fragile, and his head cannot maintain its position if moved too rapidly or forcefully.

 ## How You Can Help

Balance: Give your baby plenty of opportunities to stabilize his balance. Seat him on a pillow and allow him to hold onto you until he feels safe and secure. Challenge his balance by handing him toys, calling to him from different parts of the room so he has to turn to find you, and tossing him a soft toy to see if he can maintain his balance while trying to catch it. Be sure he's on a soft surface in case he tumbles.

Stepping: Give your baby as much assisted walking time as possible. Practice will enable him to walk when he's really ready. In the meantime he's strengthening his legs, stabilizing his balance, and learning how to take steps by alternating his feet.

Roughhousing: While your baby generally likes to engage in gross motor play that's active, physical, and enthusiastic, make sure you don't get too rough with him. Play that's too vigorous could cause whiplash-like injuries or Shaken Baby Syndrome.

Baby's Cognitive Development

Pre-Reading Skills: Your baby may be growing more attentive to books now, especially if you've been reading to him for some time. You may see him focusing his eyes on pictures that illustrate the words you're reading. He may also be following your fingers if you're using them to track the words. Watch his facial expressions for signs of excitement and comprehension.

Mealtime: Mealtime isn't just eating time for your baby; it's fun time, too. He wants to explore his food with all his senses. Make sure you have plenty of interesting toys on hand to keep him occupied and eating. Let him take a break occasionally, if necessary. A pleasurable mealtime will enhance your baby's independence and help prevent eating disorders.

Positive Reinforcement: Your baby learns positive behavior through positive reinforcement. When he does something that pleases you, let him know you appreciate it. The more you positively reinforce acceptable behaviors, the more he reproduces them.

 # How You Can Help

Pre-Reading Skills: Give your baby a chance to absorb a picture book by reading slowly, by making your voice interesting, by pointing out important pictures, and by not turning the pages too quickly. He needs time to process everything. Choose books that have large, clear illustrations and simple stories.

Mealtime: Provide your baby with fun foods to eat and fun ways to eat them. He may enjoy picking up Cheerios out of his dump truck or using his color-ful baby spoon to eat mashed potatoes. Cover him with a large plastic bib or apron so you don't have to worry about the mess. Encourage him to taste new foods, but don't be discouraged if he doesn't like them right away. Babies sometimes need time to develop a taste for a new food. Fun with food doesn't mean he can throw it or spit it, so intervene if he gets carried away.

Positive Reinforcement: Catch your baby "being good" instead of "being bad." For example, if he responds appropriately to your simple request, smile and say, "Thanks, (baby's name)" or "I appreciate that, (baby's name)." He wants to please you, and he needs guidance to know what you want.

Baby's Psychological Development

Self-Help: As your baby develops a more independent sense of self, he may begin participating in simple tasks such as dressing himself, bathing himself, and feeding himself. He may try to stick his arm through the sleeve when you're putting on his shirt, grab the wet washcloth to wipe his face, or reach for your food to have a taste.

Special Time: Set aside a special time each day to enjoy your baby. This is especially important on hectic days or when your schedule has been disrupted. Special times help you maintain a deep connection with your baby, and they encourage healthy habits that last a lifetime.

Copycat: Your baby learns many activities, behaviors, gestures, and words by watching you. If you observe him closely, you'll see how he imitates your actions during playtime. He'll try to fit something in the VCR, he'll point the remote toward the TV, he'll bend his legs to dance when he hears music, and so on.

 # How You Can Help

Self-Help: Whenever possible, give your baby the opportunity to help himself with simple tasks. Instead of fighting him while trying to dress him, watch for signs that he wants to help, then let him do as much as he can. Let him bathe himself as much as he likes and feed himself even though it's messy.

Special Time: Think about your baby's activity cycle over the course of an average day, and choose a special time that works for you. If he's especially alert right after a nap, spend half an hour or more playing closely with him. If he gets fussy or distracted, stop the activity and switch to something else. Repeat a favorite activity as long as he's having fun, introduce new ones to keep things interesting, and make an effort to make your special time together pleasurable and positive.

Copycat: Play the Copycat game with your baby. Perform a simple activity, such as clapping, and encourage him to imitate you. Switch to a new movement every few minutes and see what he does. Wave your hands, flap your arms, cover your face, pat your head, wiggle your feet, shake your head, and so on.

Week 43: Thinking

 ## Baby's Physical Development

Grasping: Your baby is getting better at using her thumb and fingers to grasp and manipulate objects. You may see her holding objects by their handles or ends as she discovers new ways of grasping.

Scribbling: Your baby may be able to grasp a non-toxic felt-tip pen in her palm and hold it much like a knife. She may make stabbing motions at whatever's in front of her, such as paper. This shows that she understands what the pen and paper are for, and she's making further attempts to control her fine motor skills.

Encouragement: As your baby practices her gross and fine motor skills, give her lots of encouragement, but don't push her. She's on her own timetable and will take the next step when she's ready. Give her plenty of opportunities to practice her skills, gain confidence, and be ready when it's time to move on.

 ## How You Can Help

Grasping: Give your baby objects to hold that have handles, stems, or graspable ends. Examples include bells, cups, wands, pots, drumsticks, flags, breadsticks, paintbrushes, and large crayons or pens. Show her how to hold the objects if she has trouble getting started.

Scribbling: To encourage your baby's pre-writing skills and enable her to gain more control over her hands and fingers, offer her a large crayon or non-toxic felt-tip pen and a large sheet of paper. Seat her in her highchair, tape the paper to the tray so it doesn't slide, and let her draw lines on the paper. You're helping her establish the foundation for artistic expression and writing.

Encouragement: While your baby is practicing a skill, use encouraging words such as, "You can do it," "Let's try," or "Let's do it again." Watch her for signs of exhaustion or irritation and stop the activity if she becomes overstimulated. Give her support without performing the task for her and set up situations in which she can succeed in small steps.

Baby's Cognitive Development

Choosing: As your baby becomes more independent, she wants to make more of her own decisions. This gives her a feeling of power and control over herself and her life, and it establishes the foundation for later decision-making skills. Try to avoid offering her choices in situations in which you have a desired response, or when her choice won't ultimately matter.

Language: Your baby is absorbing language at a rapid rate. Continue to name familiar people and objects, use simple sentences when describing things, talk to her throughout the day, add facial expressions and gestures, and take the time to listen to her "talk," so she understands how important language is.

Playthings: Playthings become even more interesting to your baby about now. She's learning how to play with more sophisticated toys appropriately, beyond simply banging them, throwing them, or chewing them. Offer her a variety of interesting toys that stimulate different parts of her development, such as large-piece puzzles, shape sorters, stacks of rings, play telephones, and so on.

 # How You Can Help

Choosing: Offer your baby choices whenever possible, so she feels as if her desires and opinions matter. Try to limit her choices, since too many options can be overwhelming at this age. Instead of offering her yes/no choices, have her choose between two things such as toys, foods, clothing items, and so on.

Language: Play language-building games with your baby. When she says a word-sound, respond to her by saying a sound that rhymes with it. For example, if she says, "goo," then say, "moo." See if she responds by repeating what you said or by coming up with another rhyming sound. If she doesn't say anything, continue with, "zoo" and so on. Playing with words makes learning language even more fun.

Playthings: Make sure your baby's playthings are age appropriate, easy to use, and safe. (They don't have parts that are sharp or can break off and be swallowed.) Toys that are too difficult for your baby usually lead to boredom or frustration. Other good toys for this age include dolls, puzzles, push toys, balls, blocks, clay, and dough.

Baby's Psychological Development

Pleasure: Your baby is no longer simply imitating the happy faces around her; she's truly experiencing joy, happiness, and satisfaction. Watch her smile when she sees someone special, accomplishes a new task, and finds a fun toy to play with.

Security: If your baby feels safe and secure in her attachment to you, she tends to reach out to others and take more chances with her skills and abilities. Be there for her when she needs you, and she'll have the confidence to explore her environment.

Play: No matter how expensive or well designed a toy may be, you are your baby's most important plaything. You stimulate all her senses, you're interactive, you're endlessly fascinating, you use language, you nurture, and you're just plain fun. Remember, you don't always need toys to play with your baby.

 How You Can Help

Pleasure: Try to shower your baby with pleasant tones throughout day by smiling, laughing, and saying things like, "I like your picture," "I'm so happy," and "This is fun!" Since she's still very sensitive to your moods, smile as much as possible around her, and remain calm and pleasant when she becomes upset, to help calm her down.

Security: If your baby is reluctant to try a new activity or go to a stranger, don't force her. That will only undermine her sense of security. She needs to reach out at her own pace. Encourage her, but avoid making her try something she's not ready to try.

Play: Think about the endless ways you can play with your baby. You may never buy a toy again! Each time you play with her, she learns physical skills, cognitive skills, and psychosocial skills. You are the most important plaything she will ever have.

Week 44: Sensing

 ## Baby's Physical Development

Sleep: Your baby's sleep patterns change as he approaches the end of his first year. A newborn sleeps an average of sixteen hours, while an eleven-month-old sleeps an average of thirteen hours. Near the end of the first year, most babies are sleeping at least six hours straight during the night, and they're taking one to two naps during the day.

Hand Exploration: By eleven months your baby has developed a lot of dexterity in his hands and fingers. He's now capable of estimating an object's size using his hands, and he can coordinate his hands to hold an object that's too big for one hand alone.

Vision: Your baby's vision is about 20/20 now, a great improvement from his newborn vision. Because of changes in his brain's neural network, he's now able to focus, track, and scan quite well.

 ## How You Can Help

Sleep: Your family schedule can influence your baby's sleep patterns to some degree, but his internal clock is also a factor in how much sleep he gets and how well he sleeps. You shouldn't try to force your baby to conform to your sleep schedule. Be sensitive to his patterns and accommodate them, if possible.

Hand Exploration: Offer your baby a toy he can easily hold with one hand. After he plays with it for a few minutes, offer him a larger toy that requires both hands to hold, and see what he does. Make sure it's an object he can manage—one that challenges him without frustrating him, such as a large ball, a loaf of bread, a pillow, or a box.

Vision: If your baby doesn't see well at a distance, doesn't track your finger well, or doesn't scan the room for a sound or toy, inform your pediatrician and have him or her do an eye exam. Your baby's binocular vision should also be improving rapidly, so his depth perception should be better.

Baby's Cognitive Development

Distinguishing Sounds: Your baby can distinguish between similar consonant sounds such as "pah" and "bah," "dah" and "tah," and "mah" and "nah." He'll soon be able to distinguish between similar vowel sounds such as "ah" and "oh."

Taste and Smell: Your baby's other senses are developing rapidly, too. His ability to distinguish various tastes and smells is at its peak at this time. He's ready to try many new foods.

Touch: Your baby's sense of touch is remarkably acute by this time. He learns a great deal from handling objects, and he distinguishes them based on temperature, size, hardness, weight, and texture.

 # How You Can Help

Distinguishing Sounds: Continue playing the rhyming game so your baby can learn how to distinguish between similar consonant sounds. Add a twist to the game by changing the vowels instead of the consonants. For example, say "mah," then say, "moh," "mee," "may," and "moo." Repeat these sounds a few times and see if your baby imitates you.

Taste and Smell: Play tasting games with your baby and watch his expressions as he tries different fruits, vegetables, and so on. Play smelling games by walking around the house and letting him smell familiar odors such as perfume, soap, coffee, baby lotion, flowers, a scented candle, and so on. Avoid foods and odors that are pungent or foul.

Touch: Collect a few items that have similar but different textures, such as fabric swatches, shoes, snacks, papers, or toys. Let your baby handle one object and describe it to him as he plays with it. Give him a similar object and tell him how it's different. As you go about your day, describe the feeling of different objects to enhance both his awareness of touch and the language to go with it.

Baby's Psychological Development

Social Referencing: Your baby continues to use you as an emotional reference point when he's in doubt about a situation or feeling. Watching his parent's expression helps him know when an activity is safe and when there's danger.

Self-Awareness: Your baby is beginning to learn the names of his body parts, and he may respond to questions about them. Soon he should be able to identify his nose, mouth, ears, and bellybutton, and eventually his hands, arms, legs, head, and body.

Security: Your baby may go through a stage in which he feels insecure even a few feet away from you. He's experiencing a push-pull dynamic in which he wants the security of his caregiver and, at the same time, wants the freedom to roam. You may find him leaving you one moment and running back the next.

 # How You Can Help

Social Referencing: Although you can influence your baby's emotional responses, be careful not to overdo it. He needs to learn what his real feelings are. For example, if he falls down, don't panic and run over to rescue him. You might make him feel worse than he really does. On the other hand, don't ignore him if he's really hurt. Wait calmly to see how he reacts, then respond appropriately.

Self-Awareness: Play games to help your baby learn his body parts, such as Head-Shoulders-Knees-and-Toes. You can also play Where's-Your-(Body Part)? Ask him, "Where's your nose?" Then point to his nose and say, "There's your nose!" Play these games in the mirror and have him find his body parts in his reflection.

Security: If your baby demonstrates push-pull behavior, give him whatever he needs. It's a developmental phase he'll eventually outgrow. Don't force him to separate if you don't have to, and allow him to cling if he needs you. He'll be more apt to deal with his ambiguous feelings if you let him work them out on his own.

Week 45: Cruising

 Baby's Physical Development

Fine Motor: As your baby's finger manipulation becomes more fine tuned, she's better able to use her pincer grasp to retrieve small items, put objects inside other objects, and take objects out of small spaces. This dexterity practice will enable her to eat without spilling, dress herself, and do many other fine motor tasks in the near future.

Sitting: Your baby is growing more adept at moving in and out of a sitting position. She's also able to turn her body while sitting and reach for an object located to her side or behind her.

Cruising: Around this time your baby may begin walking while assisted by the furniture she's holding onto. She may pull to standing, find her balance, and take a step or two using the couch for support. This is called cruising, which is the next step toward walking unassisted.

 How You Can Help

Fine Motor: Give your baby more fine motor experiences including putting small objects into egg cartons (objects she can't swallow or food items that are safe to put in her mouth), doing large-piece wooden puzzles, using a pegboard, picking objects out of containers, and finger-painting on large sheets of paper.

Sitting: Give your baby sitting challenges by placing objects near her but slightly out of her reach, so she has to change her body position in order to grasp them. Place toys at her side and behind her to get her to reach around. Place an object on the couch so she has to pull to standing in order to retrieve it.

Cruising: Set your baby in a standing position next to one end of the couch. Place a toy at the other end so she has to cruise to get it. Sit near the toy and encourage her to come and get it. Bare feet are still recommended for your baby as she learns to travel on foot.

Baby's Cognitive Development

Language: There's soon to be an explosion of language as your baby prepares to speak her first word. Parents continue to use Parentese at this time, a natural form of teaching their baby language that includes short sentences, simple vocabulary, a high-pitched voice, animated intonation, and lots of repetition. Baby talk is fine as long as you don't use it all the time. She needs to hear you speak normally, too.

Descriptive Concepts: While your baby is learning primarily concrete words (such as "doggy" and "bottle") and simple phrases (such as "Bye-bye" and "Hi!"), she's receptive to descriptions of objects and actions, such as "Big doggy!" and "Go bye-bye." She's also capable of understanding more abstract words like "dirty," "hurry," "surprise," "hungry," and "wait."

Sequential Play: While your baby seems to be playing with toys randomly, you might notice that she occasionally does things in sequence. For example, if there are blocks on the floor, she might put them back in the box one by one. This is a major step in cognitive development and organized thinking.

 # How You Can Help

Language: Your baby needs lots of repetition of familiar words in order to learn how to say them. It's especially helpful if you simplify your sentences for clarity, such as, "Do you want a bottle?" "Ready for your bottle?" or "It's time for your bottle." Enunciate clearly when you speak to her, to help her understand you better. Never correct her speech, because criticism may inhibit her language development. Simply set a good example by following the guidelines mentioned above.

Descriptive Concepts: Increase your baby's receptive vocabulary by describing objects and actions throughout the day. For example, describe what you're doing, seeing, hearing, and feeling as you clean the house, change her diaper, take a walk together, and so on.

Sequential Play: You can teach your baby sequential play by putting things in order while she watches you, by talking about what you're doing, and by showing her the steps. For example, show her how to put each block back in the box, how to take the puzzle pieces out one at a time, and so on.

Baby's Psychological Development

Positive Reinforcement: Your baby understands when you appreciate something she does, and she'll repeat the behavior if your praise and positive reinforcement continue. Remember to smile at her, laugh with her, encourage her, make frequent eye contact, and celebrate her accomplishments.

Imitation Play: Your baby learns by watching you and by imitating your actions, behaviors, facial expressions, and vocalizations. You might find her "talking" on the phone, "cooking" with your spoons and bowls, or even trying to undress herself, just like you.

Anticipation: While reading a familiar story to your baby, you may find she anticipates what's going to happen next. She may vocalize (such as, "Uh-oh!"), gesture, clap her hands, or express her excitement in some other way. Her memory is increasing, and this enables her to anticipate things.

 # How You Can Help

Positive Reinforcement: Pay attention to your baby's positive behavior and reinforce it through your body language and speech. She will effectively learn what's expected of her if you call attention to it. In other words, catch her "being good," and let her know her positive behavior is appreciated. Ignore her negative behavior as much as possible, and it will probably disappear.

Imitation Play: Give your baby opportunities to imitate your actions. Provide her with play phones, plastic bowls and spoons, dress-up clothes, pretend cosmetics, plastic keys and a steering wheel, and other adult props. This type of play helps her prepare for the real world.

Anticipation: Each time you read your baby a familiar story, include gestures and vocalizations that are easy for her to imitate. After doing this several times, give her a moment to anticipate the gestures or sounds as you read the story. She'll soon begin to anticipate nearly every page!

Week 46: Standing Alone

 ## Baby's Physical Development

Standing Alone: Around this time your baby may release his grip on your hand or the furniture and stand alone. He needs to feel stable enough to maintain his balance and confident enough to let go without fear of falling.

Walking with Minimal Support: Your baby may now be practicing walking by holding only one of your fingers rather than your whole hand. This means he's almost ready to take his first step unassisted. Practicing with minimal support is the final stage of learning how to walk.

Eating: Your baby's tastes have expanded in the past few weeks as he's tried several new foods. He may be eating much of what you normally eat, and now his food may be finely chopped instead of mashed. He may also be imitating family members' eating habits to the best of his ability. Meals are still quite messy, but he's getting better.

 ## How You Can Help

Standing Alone: Place your baby in a standing position in the middle of the room and hold one of his hands. When you feel him find his balance, slowly release your grip while keeping your hands nearby in order to catch him if he starts to fall. Practice several times a day and provide plenty of encouragement.

Walking with Minimal Support: To help your baby take the final step toward walking unassisted, have him hold only your index fingers while he's practicing. As he grows increasingly adept, release one of your fingers. If he needs something to help him feel secure and balanced, give him a toy to hold in his free hand. Practice every day, if possible.

Eating: Include your baby at the family mealtime so he can observe your behavior, join in the conversation, and socialize with everyone. If he throws food, remove the food to teach him that behavior won't be tolerated. Don't serve foods he can choke on, such as hot dog pieces, popcorn, hard candy, grapes, and peanut butter. Continue to avoid honey as well, which can cause botulism in babies.

Baby's Cognitive Development

Expanding Language: Your baby's language comprehension is now expanding to include phrases. He can probably respond appropriately to phrases like, "Want up?" "Time to eat," "Let's go bye-bye," "Daddy's home!" and "Where's doggy?"

Same and Different: Your baby is getting better at sorting his toys and other objects. He notices and compares how they're similar and different. This organizing skill leads to classifying skills that help him further sort and understand his world.

Receptive Language: Before your baby speaks his first word, he has the capacity to understand nearly fifty words and simple phases. He also has the ability to understand some words without any accompanying gestures.

 # How You Can Help

Expanding Language: Continue responding to your baby's speech and expanding it whenever possible. For example, if he attempts to say, "bottle" by saying, "ba-ba," repeat the word correctly within a phrase such as, "Want your bottle?" He's more likely to understand and respond appropriately to questions and commands, so use them frequently.

Same and Different: Set out some objects that are similar and ones that are different, such as two blocks, two balls, a cup, and a stuffed animal. Demonstrate how to sort the objects by placing the blocks together and the balls together. Use language to describe your actions, such as, "These are the same." Set the other objects apart and say, "These are different." Practice each day. Your baby will participate as he begins to understand the concepts.

Receptive Language: Identify the words and phrases your baby understands and record them in his growth and development book. You'll be surprised at how much he understands by the end of his first year!

Baby's Psychological Development

Behavior: Your baby is capable of restricting or changing his behavior to some degree. For example, if he's taught not to touch something, or if he's told, "No!" in reference to something dangerous, he may stop. He may continue to test the boundaries, but he'll often check with his parent first when he knows something is off limits. This is the beginning of self-control.

Smiling: Your baby may greet you with a smile when he sees you, and not necessarily because you've done something pleasing. He may also smile at himself in the mirror and enjoy the response. But when strangers arrive, he may withhold the smile until he feels comfortable.

Playing Games: Your baby enjoys playing with you, and he may begin initiating games instead of waiting for you to start them. He shows signs of wanting to play by imitating the action, by finding the necessary prop, by babbling the words, or by humming the song to a game.

 # How You Can Help

Behavior: When your baby does something he's not allowed to do, tell him, "No!" in a distinct voice with a matching facial expression. If he continues, remove him from the situation or remove the object. Follow through and be consistent when enforcing a restriction, so he knows a rule is not to be broken. He'll learn over time not to do something. However, try not to overuse "No!" Its effectiveness will be diminished with overuse.

Smiling: Encourage your baby's smile by smiling at him when he wakes up, when you see him during the day, and whenever you feel like it. Make smiling faces while looking in the mirror together, to show him how his face changes and to help him learn the reflection in the mirror is really him. He probably enjoys his image so much, he laughs at it, pats the mirror, or puts his mouth on the image.

Playing Games: Watch your baby for signs that he wants to play a specific game. Try to accommodate him whenever possible, to reinforce his actions. He may especially like the old favorites Gonna-Get-You, Pat-a-Cake, Peek-a-Boo, and Where's Baby?

Week 47: Walking

 ## Baby's Physical Development

Walking: Your baby may take her first step any day now. When she finally lets go and takes that step, she may fall, but your excitement will inspire her to try again. Some babies are not ready to walk until eighteen months or more, but this is still within the range of normal.

Pointing: As your baby gains more control over her fine motor movements, she begins to point at anything and everything. This gesture indicates that she recognizes objects in her environment and is trying to identify them or acquire them. She may also investigate objects by poking them with her index finger.

Climbing: When your baby becomes proficient at crawling on flat surfaces, she may attempt to crawl up stairs. She'll probably favor one leg and lead with it. She may be able to climb up fairly easily, but she often can't figure out how to get back down. Teach her to crawl down safely by staying on her belly and using her hands and feet to control her backward descent.

 ## How You Can Help

Walking: If your baby has been standing, cruising, and walking with assistance for some time now, she's probably going to walk alone soon, if she hasn't already. Give her lots of opportunities to practice her walking skills. She'll soon have enough confidence to take that first step.

Pointing: Help your baby gain more control over her fingers by demonstrating how to point. As you read a book or walk around the house with her, point to interesting things and name them. Set a few objects on the table, identify them, and ask her to point to them as you name them. Help her learn her body parts by pointing to them and naming them.

Climbing: Give your baby the opportunity to improve her gross motor skills by climbing steps. Supervise her closely and keep staircases blocked at the top and bottom when you're not practicing.

Baby's Cognitive Development

Toys: Your baby learns from the toys she plays with. She thinks about them and figures out how to manipulate them appropriately. The more toys she has, the more opportunities she has to learn new skills. But many babies prefer to play with everyday items such as plastic bowls, car keys, a loaf of bread, a box, measuring cups, and so on. These are toys, too!

Differentiation: As your baby meets more people, she continues to distinguish them by their facial details, voices, and gestures. You may find she reacts differently to different people, sometimes based on gender (she can tell most male faces from female faces) or facial features such as a mustache, glasses, or a scar.

Syllables: Your baby can probably put syllables together that sound like words, such as "dah-dah" (for daddy), "ny-ny" (for "night-night"), and so on. She's more apt to use syllables that begin with easier consonants such as "d," "g," and "n." Others, such as "m," "p," and "k," are more difficult to pronounce and are less likely to be used at this age.

 # How You Can Help

Toys: Provide your baby with a variety of playthings, so she has the opportunity to learn many different ways of thinking, manipulating, and problem solving. Don't restrict her playthings based on gender. Encourage your daughter to play with "boy" toys such as trucks and footballs, and encourage your son to play with "girl" toys such as dolls.

Differentiation: Watch how your baby reacts to different people and see if you can determine which features she responds to. Play a game of Disguise with her. One by one, add various props to your face, such as a hat, glasses, a funny nose, a wig, a mustache, and a mask. Watch her reaction to each change.

Syllables: Mom, don't be hurt if your baby says, "dada" before "mama." "Dada" is easier to say. Play syllable games with your baby by repeating sounds over and over. If she hears them frequently, she may attempt to imitate them. Don't correct her when she speaks. Simply model the sounds, and she'll pick them up before you know it.

Baby's Psychological Development

Getting Attention: Your baby will perform for you if she gets a positive reaction. She'll make funny noises, bounce up and down on her legs, or repeat other behavior that gets a laugh. She's not showing off. She's entertaining you and getting a positive response.

Taking Turns: Your baby is learning how to take turns through play. When you trade toys with her or take turns practicing a skill, she begins to understand that she'll get another turn or get her toy back. She's learning about sharing.

Separation Anxiety: Your baby may still cling a bit when you leave, but she may also be easily distracted by her new caregiver, especially if the person has something interesting to offer. You might ask your babysitter to bring fun things to distract your baby and ease the transition. It's good for her to be away from you occasionally to help promote her independence.

 # How You Can Help

Getting Attention: When your baby performs for you, be sure to show your delight by smiling, laughing, or applauding. This reinforces her behavior and enhances her self-awareness and self-esteem. Call attention to her performance by saying, "Look at (baby's name), she's dancing!" She'll love it.

Taking Turns: Help your baby learn to take turns by offering her a toy and letting her play with it for a few minutes. Then offer her another toy and take the first toy from her, if she's willing. Exchange toys again. Set your toy down and ask if you can have the toy she's holding. See if she offers it to you for a turn. Be sure to give it back.

Separation Anxiety: To ease the transition of leaving your baby, talk to her and tell her what you're doing and where you're going. Give her time to adjust to her new caregiver. Never rush out or try to sneak out. Be sure to say good-bye, and leave something special behind, if necessary, so she knows you're coming back.

Week 48: Talking

 Baby's Physical Development

Scribbling: If your baby has watched you write or draw, and if he's had the opportunity to imitate you using a crayon or non-toxic felt-tip pen, he may be able to scribble on a large sheet of paper. This is the second step in the development of pre-writing skills and artistic expression.

Standing Up: Although your baby may now be standing without support, getting himself into a standing position may still be a challenge. In time he'll be able to push or pull himself to standing without your help or that of nearby furniture.

Motor Skills: Babies tend to concentrate on one skill at a time. If he's focused on gross motor skills such as standing, cruising, and walking, he may be less apt to talk. If he focuses on fine motor skills such as grasping, scribbling, and eating, he may be less interested in gross motor skills such as walking.

 How You Can Help

Scribbling: Let your baby have a chance to use crayons and non-toxic felt-tip pens on a regular basis, and soon he'll be able to control his hand movements enough to make scribbling marks. Encourage him by drawing with him, so he can imitate your movements. Don't expect much more than scribbles for another year.

Standing Up: Help your baby practice standing up without assistance. Place him in a sitting position, then turn him over into a bear-crawl position, so his hands and feet are touching the ground but his tummy is off the floor. Then support him as he attempts to right himself into a standing position. This will take some practice—it's not easy without support—but it presents a good challenge for your baby.

Motor Skills: If your baby is concentrating on gross motor skills, give him extra time to practice fine motor skills such as doing simple puzzles, drawing on paper, working with playdough, or using a pegboard. If he's good at fine motor skills, give him more time on the floor to encourage his arm and leg movements and pre-walking skills.

Baby's Cognitive Development

First Word: Most babies say their first words around the end of the first year. Some babies speak earlier, around eight to nine months, and some wait until fourteen to eighteen months. But usually by the end of the first year, most babies say a word that has meaning for them. The word may not be perfectly enunciated, but you can tell it has meaning from your baby's expression, gestures, and repetition.

Sign Language: Most babies learn language faster when words are accompanied by signs or gestures. A visual representation offers your baby a concrete picture of the word, which helps him learn it faster. Signs will not reduce your baby's speech, they will increase it.

Deferred Imitation: Your baby is apt to copy a behavior or action he has seen recently. This is called deferred imitation. He may imitate something you have done or act out a scene from his favorite TV show. Deferred imitation leads to imaginary play, another big step in cognitive development.

 # How You Can Help

First Word: Repeat your baby's first word back to him to reinforce it, then begin to expand on it. For example, if he says, "juice," say, "Do you want juice?" This will increase his receptive language and eventually his expressive language. If you ignore his first words, he may stop trying to say them. Listen carefully for this important step.

Sign Language: Pick up a book on baby sign language or develop your own signs that your baby understands. Keep them simple and clear. Use the sign each time you say the word, and soon he'll learn the word. Begin with simple words like "doggy" (pat your leg), "milk" (squeeze your fist), or "up" (point up).

Deferred Imitation: After you read a book or watch a TV show with your baby, take out some props and imitate a scene from the book or show. Encourage him to join in the play. You might also find an object that appears in the book and see how he plays with it.

Baby's Psychological Development

Naming: As your baby begins to speak his first words, he'll soon refer to you as "mama" or "dada" or some variation. At first he may simply play with these words to elicit your response. Eventually he'll use them appropriately, calling you when he needs you.

Emotions: By the end of the first year, your baby is capable of a wider range of emotions including jealousy, fear, anger, surprise, excitement, and guilt. He's expanding his emotional range and fine-tuning his feelings—a big leap in his emotional development. His emotional intensity will increase, too. You'll see big hugs and kisses when he feels loving, stormy tantrums when he's angry or frustrated, and face-hiding when he's embarrassed.

Friends: Your baby prefers the company of people his own age, with few exceptions (such as you). He feels comfortable with his peers. At this age he copies their behavior, tries to talk to them, plays with their toys, and generally attempts to interact with them.

 # How You Can Help

Naming: Respond to your baby with delight when he calls your name. As he begins to use it appropriately, make every effort to figure out what he wants. Once you do, give him the language that describes his request and your response. Continue to use the names of family members and friends. He'll soon be naming them, too.

Emotions: Try to understand your baby's emotional expressions, and use the words that describe his emotions. If he's angry about something, don't ignore it or deny it. Accept it and give him the words to help him express his emotions through language instead of action.

Friends: Give your baby the opportunity to interact with children his own age. This first stage of play is called "parallel play," in which babies play side by side, enjoy the same toys, and generally interact in a friendly way.

Week 49: Thoughtfulness

 ## Baby's Physical Development

Walking Backward: If your baby is standing well and beginning to take those first steps, she may also try to take a step backward, a complex task that's more accidental than deliberate at this point. She'll soon be walking backward, sideways, and eventually running!

Sitting with Ease: Your baby is probably sitting down with ease now, instead of dropping to the ground without control. She may use furniture to help her, or she may bend her knees and sit without assistance. She may also be able to get back up again without assistance.

Block Tower: Your baby's hand control and finger control are increasing rapidly. Around this time she may be able to build a short block tower (about three blocks). Her placement may not be perfect, but she knows she's supposed to stack the blocks, and she makes the effort to get one on top of another.

 ## How You Can Help

Walking Backward: To encourage your baby to try new ways of walking, give her push-and-pull toys to experiment with. A push toy may help steady her as she practices walking. It may even enable her to walk faster. Pull toys will encourage her to walk backward.

Sitting with Ease: To help your baby practice sitting and getting up, play a game of Ring-around-the-Rosy. Place her in a standing position and hold both her hands, so the two of you form a ring-around-the-rosy circle. Then sing the song. When it's time to fall, squat and sit down, and have her imitate you. Repeat the song, but when it's time to fall, let go of her hands, and see if she sits down on her own. Spot her in case she loses control.

Block Tower: Give your baby the opportunity to control her fine motor movements by building a block tower. Use medium-size blocks that are easier to manage and less likely to tumble. Show her how to stack them, then let her try. If the tower falls or if she knocks it over, say, "Uh-oh!" Then smile and build it again.

Baby's Cognitive Development

Sorting: As neurons in your baby's brain continue to differentiate, she becomes better able to sort and classify the objects in her world. At first she makes gross generalizations, calling all four-legged creatures "doggy." Soon she'll be able to distinguish a dog from a cat and other animals, as she better understands their similarities and differences.

Identifying: Your baby can identify several familiar objects by pointing to them when you say their names. She may also say the names, "doggy," "daddy," or "bottle." She's able to recognize more objects than she can name, since her receptive language is much more developed than her expressive language.

Animal Sounds: As your baby is learning more words, she's also learning to identify animal sounds. She can tell the difference between words and animal noises and she can use them appropriately in a limited capacity.

 # How You Can Help

Sorting: Give your baby the opportunity to sort things by providing different groups of objects that are similar yet different. For example, find two stuffed dogs and two stuffed cats. See if she can sort the cats from the dogs. Identify the animals and show her how they're different, if necessary. Do the same using food and non-food items, baby clothes and adult clothes, kitchen items and bath items, and so on.

Identifying: Name objects around the house as your baby interacts with them. The words will have more meaning for her if she hears them in an appropriate context. Then play an identification game with her. Set out three familiar items and ask her, "Where's the ball?" She should point to the correct object if she recognizes it.

Animal Sounds: Make animal noises that match toy animals or pictures of animals. Let your baby imitate the noises after you make them. Play a game by making an animal sound and having her pick out the animal. Hold up an animal and ask her what sound it makes.

Baby's Psychological Development

Security Blanket: As your baby learns to distinguish various objects, animals, and people, she may experience increased stranger anxiety. A security blanket or other lovey may play an important role now, so let her keep it nearby when she needs it.

Discipline: As your baby becomes more independent, she begins to disobey some of your rules. This means she's thinking for herself, certainly not a bad thing. She needs to feel free in order to learn about herself and her world, but she also needs limitations in order to feel safe. Over time she'll internalize your guidance and discipline and be able to control her behavior. Until then it's your job to teach her what's acceptable and what's not by guiding her, not by punishing her.

Overstimulation: Excitement that's not part of your baby's daily routine (a birthday party, for example) can sometimes be overwhelming. If she becomes overstimulated, she may cry, throw a tantrum, or withdraw. She'll need a break from the activity to calm herself down.

 # How You Can Help

Security Blanket: A security blanket or other lovey gives your baby more independence, not less. Without it she may be afraid to experience new things or venture out on her own. She may use a blanket, toy, pacifier, or one of your belongings to help her feel secure under stress. As she gets older and learns to cope, allow her to keep some portion of her lovey with her, if she needs it, such as a piece of her blanket, a smaller version of her toy, or a picture of you.

Discipline: When you discipline your baby, you essentially guide her toward appropriate behavior. When she tests your boundaries or asserts herself, use positive discipline techniques such as redirection, intervention, repetition, role modeling, and explanation. The essence of good discipline is teaching, not punishing.

Overstimulation: To reduce the possibility of your baby disintegrating emotionally during an exciting event, talk to her frequently and give her lots of breaks from the activity. Be aware that she may have trouble coping with more stimulation than normal.

Week 50: Imagination

 Baby's Physical Development

Size: At one year the average baby weighs twenty-two pounds and reaches thirty inches in height. He has tripled his birth weight and grown ten inches, almost an inch a month. The one-year-old's head makes up one-fourth of his body length, compared to the adult head, which is one-eighth of body length. The one-year-old's legs make up one-fourth of his body length, while adult legs are one-half of body length.

Pincer Grasp: As your baby continues to master his pincer grasp, he's probably able to pick up all kinds of things buried in the carpet, lying on the floor, and spread over his highchair tray. His ability to coordinate his thumb and index finger is improving rapidly.

Turning Pages: When you read to your baby, he probably wants to turn the pages. Encourage this participation by all means, but offer assistance if he's having trouble or tearing the pages. He'll soon be able to turn the pages with his fingers instead of his palm, which should help prevent tears.

 How You Can Help

Size: It's critical that your baby receive good nutrition to supply his body and brain with the nutrients they need to reach their full potential. He should be eating many solids by now, still taking plenty of milk, and getting lots of exercise to ensure proper growth and development.

Pincer Grasp: Continue to give your baby lots of opportunities to practice his pincer grasp. Offer him bits of food and small toys to pick up and play with. Make sure you supervise him closely so he doesn't swallow anything he shouldn't.

Turning Pages: Continue using board books so your baby can practice turning pages without tearing them. If you're reading a soft-page picture book and he accidentally tears a page, say, "Uh-oh!" and try not to get angry. He's doing the best he can. Repair the page to show him it's important not to tear. He should soon be able handle these books without tearing them.

Baby's Cognitive Development

Imagination: Along with deferred imitation, your baby will begin to show more imagination through simple dramatic play. He may copy a sibling's style of play without really understanding what he's doing, but soon he'll be pretending, acting out scenes, and dressing up in character.

Goal-Directed Behavior: Your baby is doing more goal-directed activities as he approaches his first birthday. Purposeful behavior is another step in cognitive growth. His cause-and-effect, problem-solving, and classification skills are also improving rapidly.

Experimentation: As your baby's goal-directed behavior increases, his thinking becomes more creative. He begins experimenting with objects in his world to find out more about them. With each new discovery, he builds on what he's already learned.

 # How You Can Help

Imagination: To help your baby increase his imagination, play games that involve props and dress-up clothes. Let him wear gloves or a hat and see if he acts differently. Give him toys that stimulate dramatic play, such as dolls he can nurture, cars he can pretend to drive, and playdough he can transform into different shapes.

Goal-Directed Behavior: Watch your baby's behavior to see if you can figure out what he wants when he makes noises, reaches for something, or gestures. If he cries when you need to take a toy away, he's demonstrating goal-directed behavior by wanting to continue playing with the toy. Reduce his annoyance by giving him something else fun to play with.

Experimentation: Offer your baby opportunities to experiment. Allow him to take objects apart, examine them thoroughly, and put them back together in different ways. Big Legos appropriate for his age are an excellent tool. Watch him while he's handling something new, in case it comes apart, breaks, or frustrates him. He can explore smaller items safely as long as you supervise him carefully.

Baby's Psychological Development

Temperament: If you made a list of your baby's personality characteristics in his early weeks or months, check it now to see if they've remained the same throughout his first year. Most babies maintain the same temperament from birth.

Touch: Your baby still likes to be touched, massaged, caressed, and carried, but he also wants to separate from you when he's ready to explore. He may squirm out of your lap, arch his back when he wants down, or fuss if you hold him when he's not in the mood.

Self-Awareness: Your baby is already aware that he's separate from you, and while this causes him some concern at times, it also excites him and helps him understand his individuality. He should recognize his toys, clothes, and reflection in the mirror.

 # How You Can Help

Temperament: Most experts believe you can't do much to change your baby's temperament, since it's primarily innate. But if there are aspects of his personality that cause problems, such as being extremely slow to warm up or being overly emotional, you can be sensitive to his needs, reinforce positive behavior, and attempt to calm or change his negative behavior over time.

Touch: Although your baby may try to squirm out of your arms, it's still important to hold him and show him physical affection. Find ways to interact with him physically if he doesn't like to cuddle. He may prefer roughhousing, vigorous massage, or playing body-awareness games such as Head-Shoulders-Knees-and-Toes.

Self-Awareness: Continue to let your baby look at himself in the mirror. His reflection never stops being fascinating to him. Use his name a lot, let him know his toys belong to him, and occasionally allow him to pick out what he wants to wear.

Week 51: Independence

 ## Baby's Physical Development

On the Move: Your baby may now be walking fairly well, or she may still pre-fer to crawl. Either way, she's on the move, and there's probably no stopping her. The world is opening up to her in new and exciting ways, and she can't wait to get where she's going, even if she doesn't know where it is!

Reflexes: Some of your baby's reflexes have disappeared or will disappear soon, such as her stepping reflex, rooting reflex, heat-regulating reflex, swim-ming reflex, and Babinski's reflex (which makes the big toe flex upward and the other toes fan out when the sole of the foot is stroked firmly). She may still startle and cry when surprised, and her grasp reflex may still be somewhat active, but these and other reflexes will soon vanish.

Squatting: As your baby's leg muscles become stronger and more coordi-nated, she may be able to move from standing to squatting and back again. This enables her to walk a few steps, squat down to pick up a toy or examine an object, and move on.

 ## How You Can Help

On the Move: Let your baby practice her gross motor skills as much as pos-sible. Make sure to thoroughly baby-proof first, then give her the run of the house or yard. If there are too many restrictions on her movement, or if she's placed in a playpen, infant seat, or highchair for long periods, her gross motor development may be delayed.

Reflexes: As your baby's reflexes disappear, they are replaced by deliberate actions and behaviors. These are frequently awkward at first, but they become smoother as her muscle control improves. Try to provide her with abundant opportunities to practice deliberate movements through interactive and soli-tary play.

Squatting: Encourage your baby to squat by placing toys in the area where she's walking. If she doesn't try squatting spontaneously, she may need to imi-tate the movement, so demonstrate it for her a few times.

Baby's Cognitive Development

Searching: Your baby reaches another cognitive milestone when she begins to search for a toy or object without needing to see you hide it. She may remember where a toy was last seen or is regularly kept.

Shapes: At this age your baby begins to distinguish basic shapes. Squares and circles come first, then triangles. This is another big cognitive milestone that improves object differentiation, classification, and sorting skills.

Listening: Your baby distinguishes more and more sounds as she experiences them. She'll soon be able to identify a sound and locate it quickly and accurately. She can even distinguish similar sounds such as a doorbell ringing, a telephone ringing, and a cell phone ringing.

 # How You Can Help

Searching: Now that your baby understands object permanence fairly well, you can play a new game with her. Hide a toy in a familiar location in her playroom while she's not there. Bring her into the room and ask, "Where's the (toy)?" She may search with her eyes first, then begin to hunt in familiar spots to locate it. If she has difficulty, give her some clues by pointing to or revealing part of the toy.

Shapes: Give your baby toys designed in basic shapes, so she can become familiar with the concepts of circles, squares, and triangles. You can cut these shapes out of sponge material (make sure the material is tough enough so it can't be bitten off and choked on), felt, or even bread. Identify the shapes while she's playing with them, and soon she'll be able to identify them herself.

Listening: Create a listening game for your baby by collecting small containers such as medicine bottles or small boxes. Place noise-making objects inside the containers and seal them so she can't open them. You might choose beads, seeds, bells, tiny stones, and so on. Shake the containers, then name the contents for her. After shaking all the containers and naming all the contents, ask her, "Where are the (objects)?" See if she chooses the right container. You can also make pairs of containers with matching contents and see if she can match the sounds.

Baby's Psychological Development

Family Resemblance: If you haven't noticed them already, you may begin to see behavioral tendencies in your baby that resemble yours or your partner's. Personality tendencies such as activity level, sociability, emotionality, adaptability, distractibility, and attention span may be traceable to you, since they're genetically influenced.

Meaningful Communication: As your baby comes to appreciate the power and efficiency of language, she's more likely to use simple words and gestures to communicate her needs and thoughts. She still babbles randomly and plays with sounds, but her linguistic expressions are becoming increasingly goal-directed.

Assistance: Your baby knows how to use her parents to help her solve problems, retrieve objects she can't reach, open containers, see up high, and do other tasks. She appreciates your ability to do things she can't and she asks for your help when she needs you. Make sure you listen carefully to figure out what she's asking.

 # How You Can Help

Family Resemblance: Although traits in your baby can sometimes be attributed to genetic influence, much of her temperament and personality will be unique to her. In addition to her genetic makeup, she's influenced by her gender, birth order, number of kids in the family, economic situation, cultural environment, health, and so on. These play significant roles in shaping her personality.

Meaningful Communication: Try to understand your baby's vocalizations and gestures to keep her from getting frustrated when she tries to communicate. When she's trying to say something you don't understand, listen to her carefully, ask her questions, point to objects, and use different words to help her make herself understood.

Assistance: Your baby understands that you're her helpmate, so offer her assistance when she needs it. First encourage her to find ways to help herself, then help her out if she can't do it. If you teach her how to help herself, she'll soon be able to perform tasks without much assistance. This will increase her independence and self-esteem.

Week 52: Looking Ahead

 ## Baby's Physical Development

Gross Motor Skills: Your baby will continue to make rapid gains in gross motor development. Within the next year, he'll be using his arms, legs, and body to run, jump, hop, climb, roll, and do tricks. He'll be walking smoothly and mastering most large-muscle activities.

Fine Motor Skills: Your baby's pudgy fingers will slim down in the next few months, enabling his dexterity and fine motor skills to improve. He'll be able to draw shapes, put on and take off clothes, and eat without making a big mess. He'll be able to perform other small-muscle tasks such as playing with pegboards, handling small blocks, doing more complicated puzzles, and exploring more sophisticated "manipulatives."

Growth: By the time your baby is two years old, he'll be half as tall as the average adult, and his weight will be evenly distributed throughout his growing body. He'll continue to experience growth spurts in which he shoots up and fills out more rapidly than usual. His activity level will peak in the next year or so, so be prepared for a busy toddler.

 ## How You Can Help

Gross Motor Skills: Continue to let your baby explore his environment. Take him to the park, the playground, and a variety of other places so he can challenge his skills and expand his abilities. Give him various toys to stimulate his gross motor development, such as a wagon, scooter, play car, jungle gym, and large balls and blocks.

Fine Motor Skills: Let your baby experience new activities and materials that improve his fine motor skills, such as coloring, finger painting, brush painting, clay, and other arts and crafts. Let him try to brush his teeth, eat with a fork, do finger plays, and turn the pages of his favorite books.

Growth: Try to provide your baby with good nutrition and don't worry about his picky eating habits. He'll continue to grow and be healthy if you provide the essentials. Most toddlers prefer to eat several small meals throughout the day, rather than a few large meals.

Baby's Cognitive Development

Thinking: In the next year your baby's brain will increase in size and capacity, and he'll make tremendous strides in cognitive development. He'll be solving problems throughout the day, analyzing cause and effect, improving his classification skills, and thinking concretely about the world around him.

Language: By eighteen months your baby will probably have an expressive vocabulary of fifty words. At that age he'll be a word sponge, learning five to ten new words a day by the end of the second year. He'll begin speaking in short sentences, using correct grammar and syntax, and understanding most of the rules of speech.

Learning: Your baby will apply his growing knowledge to new objects and activities, and he'll continue to apply previous information to new experiences. He learns concepts by manipulating and sensing objects, repeating actions, imitating behavior, listening to explanations, playing with others, and so on.

 # How You Can Help

Thinking: Give your baby lots to play with, so he can continue to improve his cognitive skills. He'll enjoy puzzles, books, toys that come apart and go together, nesting toys, stacking toys, and playthings with lots of buttons, levers, and knobs to manipulate.

Language: Keep up the "conversations" with your baby. Talk to him, share your thoughts, and listen to him respond. Read to him, provide him with new adventures so he can increase his vocabulary through experience, and let him scribble so can begin to learn the connection between writing, reading, and language.

Learning: Help your baby learn by asking him questions, pointing out interesting aspects of objects and activities, giving him time to complete tasks, offering him new experiences, and so on.

Baby's Psychological Development

Self-Esteem: Your baby will feel good about himself as he gets to know his abilities, his likes and dislikes, and what makes him special. Good self-esteem is crucial to self-confidence, which helps him succeed in life.

Social Relationships: Your baby enjoys being around other children, especially those near his age. He also loves your company. He learns a lot from watching you, listening to you, and interacting with you. The ability to form meaningful friendships and social relationships helps ensure long-term happiness and success.

Birthday Party: Your baby's first birthday is an important milestone, as much for you as for him. He doesn't understand what it means to be one year old, but he does understand that something special is happening, that he's the star, and that the gift wrap and frosting are more fun than the presents and cake.

 # How You Can Help

Self-Esteem: To enhance your baby's self-esteem, offer him choices so he feels more in control of his life. Letting him make decisions will give him a real sense of power. Praise him when he behaves appropriately or accomplishes tasks independently. High self-esteem correlates with long-term happiness and success.

Social Relationships: Invite parents to bring their babies over to play with your baby, or join a playgroup or baby gym to give him opportunities to interact with other babies. Don't let your life get so busy that you don't have time to play with him often. Your relationship with your baby is the foundation for all his other relationships. It creates an attachment with you that will last forever.

Birthday Party: Keep the party short, invite mostly relatives and close friends, try to include a few other babies, and let older siblings participate in planning and enjoying the party. For more specific ideas, check out my book *Baby Birthday Parties.*

Index

The Toddler's Busy Book
The Preschooler's Busy Book
The Children's Busy Book

by Trish Kuffner

These books contain 365 activities (one for each day of the year) for your children, using things found around the home. The books show parents and day-care providers how to

- prevent boredom during even the longest stretches of bad weather with ideas for indoor play, kitchen activities, and arts-and-crafts projects;

- save money by making your own paints, play dough, craft clays, glue, paste, and other arts-and-crafts supplies;

- stimulate a child's natural curiosity with fun reading, math, and science activities.

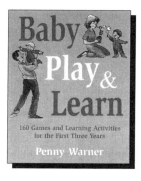 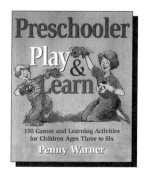

Baby Play & Learn
Preschooler Play & Learn

by Penny Warner

Child-development expert Penny Warner offers ideas for games and activities that will provide hours of developmental learning opportunities and fun for babies and preschoolers. Both books include

- bulleted lists of skills that your child learns through play;

- step-by-step instructions for each game and activity;

- illustrations demonstrating how to play the games.

Also from Meadowbrook Press

✦ *When You Were a Baby*
This one-of-a-kind board book is the only baby record book designed with a die-cut hole that enables parents to prominently feature baby's photograph on every page, with colorful illustrations showing such personal landmarks as birth, crawling, first bath, first word, first birthday, and more. The fun illustrations capture each milestone in a warm yet humorous way.

✦ *When You Were One*
Personalize landmark events in your child's early life, such as saying the first sentence, drawing the first picture, going down a slide, and much more. This board book with a die-cut hole allows a photo of your child to be visible in each colorful illustration that captures each memorable moment. With fill-in-the-blank sections, parents can record all the details of their one-year-old's milestones.

✦ *Healthy Food for Healthy Kids*
A practical guide to selecting and preparing healthy meals for kids and teaching healthy attitudes toward food. More than just a cookbook, this is a user-friendly book with real-world advice for parents who want their children to eat better.

✦ *Feed Me! I'm Yours*
Parents love this easy-to-use, economical guide to making baby food at home. More than 200 recipes cover everything a parent needs to know about teething foods, nutritious snacks, and quick, pleasing lunches.

✦ *First-Year Baby Care*
One of the leading baby-care books to guide you through your baby's first year, with complete information on the basics of baby care, including bathing, diapering, medical facts, and feeding your baby. Includes step-by-step illustrated instructions to make finding information easy, newborn screening and immunization schedules, breastfeeding information for working mothers, expanded information on child-care options, and reference guides to common illnesses.

✦ *Practical Parenting Tips*
The number-one selling collection of helpful hints for parents with babies and small children, containing 1,001 parent-tested tips for dealing with diaper rash, nighttime crying, toilet training, temper tantrums, traveling with tots, and so on. Parents will learn to save time, trouble, and money.

**We offer many more titles written to delight, inform, and entertain.
To order books with a credit card or browse our full
selection of titles, visit our web site at:**

www.meadowbrookpress.com

or call toll-free to place an order, request a free catalog, or ask a question:

1-800-338-2232

Meadowbrook Press • 5451 Smetana Drive • Minnetonka, MN • 55343